TODD SYLVESTER

I AM
RECOVERED

A SIMPLE STORY OF OVERCOMING ADDICTION

Published by Todd Sylvester Inspires, LLC.

Design and Layout by Frank Day

In association with:
Elite Online Publishing
63 East 11400 South #230
Sandy, UT 84070
EliteOnlinePublishing.com

ISBN: 978-1513655765

Table of Contents

Introduction

I have worked as a life coach and motivational speaker for the past 25 years. Throughout that time, I've had one goal: to help free my clients from faulty beliefs that limit their growth while increasing overall awareness. These limiting beliefs take many forms: irrational thoughts, faulty reasoning, and negative schemas are only a few. Whatever the thinking error happens to be, they all stem from the same underlying problem: the inability to control our thoughts.

Bad thinking is the real epidemic in today's culture. It always leads to extended sadness, grief, stress, anxiety and any other negative emotion you can imagine. We all struggle with unhealthy thinking-some more than others. My own early thinking habits led to several years of depression and anxiety. And like many adolescents, I discovered that drugs and alcohol numbed the torment. I lived the life of an addict for years.

I am no longer an addict. I am no longer "in recovery." I have grown through that portion of my life, and the principles that helped change my life will work for everyone. I have seen it time and time again with my own eyes. It works for everyone.

This is the story of where my journey began. Looking back, I wouldn't change a thing. This book wasn't written to blame, but to explain. Like all parents, mine did the best they knew how, and I wouldn't be who I am without their influence and support.

My hope is that this story and the principles found inside the book will inspire and help you remember who you are, who you've always been, and that there is nothing wrong with you.

Even the bad experiences are good.

I assure you that my personal story is 100% true. More importantly, the principles discussed are 100% true. They have the power to change lives.

Thank you for reading.

TSylvtr

Foreword

The world is full of self-help books. This one is a little different. If you pay attention, you'll see why. Most self-help books have a common, very obvious goal – to help ... yourself. I mean there's not a lot of room for interpretation there. And when you are motivated to help yourself, you tend to focus a lot on yourself, the goals you can accomplish, the power or status you can gain, the money you can make. It feels good to do things for ourselves, and in balance, it's fine. We learn a new skill, master a sport or a hobby, make progress toward our goals and it feels great, as it should!

Here's the problem. All those things – our individual, self-focused accomplishments are short term hits. They don't last. Think about it. Are you still talking about the New Year's goal you achieved 5 years ago? No! It's gone and you're on to something else. So in order to keep that feeling going, you have to keep doing things for yourself so you can keep getting those short-term hits that keep you feeling good. Again, in balance, there's nothing wrong with helping yourself, but all it can ever be is a series of short-term hits. And it's only one side of the coin.

There's another side of the coin that is equally important. And that's what makes this self-help book a little different. It takes "self-help" and elevates it to "help others". The entire purpose of improving self is so that we can share that better version of ourselves with the world around us – with the other human beings who need the gifts we naturally offer. And yes, we all have a gift to give. When we find the right balance, we can do two very important things. We can improve ourselves and better understand who we are at our core. Who we are at our natural best. Then, with that understanding of self, and the gift we have to give, we can live our lives intentionally, sharing that gift with the people around us.

And that (what we do for others) is what brings lasting fulfillment beyond a short-term self-serving happiness hit. That is what breeds connection. That is what breeds love for self and others. That is what breeds empathy. That is what makes life worth living when we're wondering what there is to live for.

- David Mead
Co-author of *Find Your WHY* and Igniter at Simon Sinek, Inc.

Chapter One
"Growing Up"

"We spend our whole childhood wanting to grow up faster, and our entire adult life wanting to go back to the simplicity of being a kid again."

- Unknown

Everyone has a unique story, if you look closely enough. From the child growing up in Malaysia surrounded by elephants to the kid being raised in the United States surrounded by stray dogs, we lead incredible lives. No matter where we're from or who we are, we all have a fascinating story. The book you're about to read is my story.

The house I grew up in was pretty standard: a 4-bedroom, 2-bathroom split-level nestled against the Wasatch Mountains near Salt Lake City, Utah. My family was also pretty standard - with two married parents and three kids, we weighed in at right above the U.S. average of 2.44 children per couple. (No elephants anywhere.)

I had good parents who were generous with their love and affection. They were comfortable saying the words "I love you," and hugs, kisses, and high fives were commonplace in our home. But organized religion was taboo in our family. We didn't talk about it, we didn't prioritize it, and we sure as hell didn't participate in it. Religion wasn't the only topic that was taboo, though—my family didn't talk about big issues at all. Drugs, alcohol, sex, politics-all these topics were typically sidestepped. And because my family avoided these important discussions, I was completely na1ve about these topics when I encountered them at school or in life outside my home. My education regarding alcohol, drugs, and even adolescence in general came from my friends and from a regular diet of media along with pop culture.

Both my parents worked hard—my dad as manager of a grocery store and my mom in the real estate business-but that's not to say that they didn't like to have fun. They knew how to party, and their gatherings were legendary—especially in Salt Lake City, where people just didn't throw the kind of events my parents did.

My dad was always the life of these parties, and he always had a glass in his hand. As a little kid, I didn't know what was in the glass, but I was shrewd enough to notice that whatever it was seemed to make him more popular with his friends.

Mom wasn't much of a drinker at first. But her alcohol consumption gradually increased as she tried to keep up with my dad and fit in with his group. The same was true for smoking. My dad encouraged, even pushed, my mom to smoke her first cigarette, which led to an 18-year nicotine addiction on her part. My dad's mentality was, "Have a drink, have a cigarette-and then stop." And because of his thinking, he *could* stop. My mom, on the other hand, had more of an "all or nothing" mentality. Once she started a behavior, she found it difficult to limit herself. She had the mentality that a lot of addicts have: If I'm going to do something, I'm doing it all the way. I eventually learned that I was a lot like my mom in this respect.

Eventually, I figured out what was in my dad's glass. Since both my parents worked during the day, my brother and I were home alone quite a bit. Even when we were in elementary school, it wasn't a big deal for us to come home in the afternoon and explore the wet bar, which we knew was the source of whatever was in my dad's glass. We were kids who wanted to be grown-ups, so we'd pour whatever we found in that little wet bar and start sipping on it.

I never got drunk or wasted or anything, but the rush of doing something sneaky and grown-up was intoxicating. We'd leave the scene of the crime with our little lips burning and the feeling that we'd gotten away with something, and then we'd come back the next day and do it all over again. I always thought that was kind of cool-and of course we never told our parents.

Isn't it interesting what we pick up as kids? In sixth grade, I developed a bit of a crush on a girl at school named Amy. She was beautiful, and I wanted to ask her to "go with me." That was the fad back then, and socially, that's what you did when you had a crush on somebody. Before asking her this important question, I had the idea to take a sip from one of my dad's liquor bottles—you know, to bolster my courage. Did I learn this by observing Mom become more social and less inhibited after drinking a little at one of her parties? I don't know.

What I did know was right where Dad kept the alcohol. My young mind somehow saw drinking alcohol as something to do in order to calm down or to boost my courage. I thought that the alcohol would somehow help me not be nervous about calling Amy and confessing that I liked her. Turns out I was right. After taking an extra-large sip from a particularly fancy-looking bottle, I called her. The conversation went as smoothly as I'd hoped it would, and she ended up being my girlfriend for a time—I even kissed her on the cheek!

After that initial alcohol-fueled social success at the ripe old age of twelve, I began sneaking larger and larger amounts of liquor from my parents' wet bar. Nobody was the wiser because there was so much alcohol in the house—the closet from which my parents stocked the wet bar contained so much alcohol that it looked like the inside of a liquor store. To me, this was normal.

Learning about my parents' drinking habits wasn't the only education I gained as a kid. I also learned from a very young age that my parents, especially my dad, were passionate about sports. Intuitively, I understood that playing sports would be a great way to connect with Dad. We talked sports all the time, and not only one or two sports—my sister, brother and I were expected to be knowledgeable about every sport. And as we grew older, we were expected to not only know about sports but also to play them well. "Can't is a four-letter word" was a common phrase from Dad, so we learned to play sports with the expectation being that we would be better than average. Soccer, baseball, gymnastics, football, basketball—you name it, we played it. This seemed to thrill my dad; the better we played, the happier he seemed. We learned that excelling at sports would earn us Dad's approval.

Looking back, my brother and sister seemed merely to endure this part of life in our home. I, on the other hand, thrived on it. I loved the way my family seemed to connect over sports; we seemed like a family when we talked about, watched or played sports. It was not uncommon on Sundays to find my dad watching two different football games on two different TVs, while listening to a third game on the radio. He lived and breathed sports and wanted his kids to feel that same kind of passion.

As I began to play sports myself, Dad didn't hold his breath hoping that I would practice-he expected me to practice. In fact, sports was so valued in our home that my parents didn't even require me to have a job after school or during the summers as long as I was practicing a sport. As I got into my high school years, it became apparent that I had a little talent, and my dad began to see college and scholarship potential in me. At the time, I thought this was wonderful, and I was excited that my dad was so involved in my sports activities. Later, though, this focus on scholarships and college play came back to slap me upside my head. More on that ahead.

So far as talent was concerned, I wasn't what you'd call a "gifted" athlete; that was my brother. But what I lacked in natural talent, I made up for in sheer determination. When I was around 13 years old, I really threw my dad a curve ball by announcing that I wanted to focus all my energy on one sport: basketball. My dad didn't like that idea much at all and tried to discourage me from quitting the other sports, but my mind was made up.

My "all or nothing" attitude was beginning to take shape and manifest itself, and I couldn't be swayed. When my dad finally realized that I was not going to change my mind, he poured a concrete basketball court on the side of our house so that I could practice. I guess he figured this would be more beneficial to me than practicing in my bedroom by throwing balled-up socks into my clothes hamper, as I had been doing.

By the time I was in the eighth grade, I was fully invested in my sport of choice. In ninth grade, I made the freshman basketball team at Brighton High School. I was a skinny little runt—one of the shortest kids on the team. And because there were taller, better kids on the team, I spent a lot of time on the bench. In fact, the coach generally only put me in the game at the very end, and then only if we were killing the other team. This frustrated me.

I knew there was nothing I could do about my height, but I was determined to practice my way to a higher skill level. I was obsessed with basketball and was out on the court 24/7-at least it felt that way. I practiced two to three hours every day, rain or shine. Even when it snowed, I shoveled off the court and kept practicing.

Our poor neighbors sometimes called the house begging my parents to PLEASE make me stop bouncing the ball, but my dad and I were unfazed by our neighbors' complaints. Our goal was for me to play professional basketball, so I just kept practicing.

Of course, in the short term, I wanted to get more playing time on my high school team and eventually a college scholarship, but what I truly spent hours daydreaming about was playing in the NBA.

Chapter 2
"Trust Me, You're Gonna Love It"

"Every addiction stems from an unconscious refusal to face and move through your own pain."

- Eckhart Tolle

Ever been able to pinpoint the exact moment your life changed forever? Well, I can. It was the end of our ninth-grade basketball season, toward the end of my freshman year. Gary, a friend from school, invited me to go camping with his family over a long holiday weekend. I really wanted to go, and somehow I managed to justify taking a break from practicing. My parents agreed that I could go; none of us had any idea that everything was about to change.

Friday morning, we set off for Bear Lake in Gary's family's Chevy Blazer. It was close to a three-hour trip with Gary and me crammed in the back, so by the time we reached the lake, I was ready to get out of that car! I clearly recall driving around the last bend in the road before finally getting a look at Bear Lake's famous turquoise water.

My legs were stiff and cramped, so I was eager to get out of the car, stretch, and start exploring. But as everyone started to pile out of the car, Gary held me back. "Wait a minute," he whispered. "What's going on?" I whispered back. He gripped my arm and hissed, "Just wait a minute!" I thought he had some kind of secret to tell me, so I eagerly waited.

When we were the only two left in the Blazer, Gary grabbed his backpack and pulled out a quarter-ounce of weed. Man, I'd never seen anything like it before. I had to ask him what it was. "It's pot," he said, looking at me like I was an idiot. "We're gonna smoke it, and you're gonna love it. Trust me—you're gonna love it!"

As naïve as it sounds now, 14-year-old me had no idea what pot was. I did know, though, that Gary was my friend, and I wanted him to accept me. Also, I was the type of kid who was always up for an adventure, so naturally my response was, "Sure, let's do it!" Gary and I hopped out of the Blazer and, trying to look nonchalant, snuck into the forest out of sight of his family. He fired up the pipe, took a hit, and passed it to me. Initially, I was unimpressed. Nothing really happened. I didn't feel any different. I certainly didn't feel the euphoria that I had been promised. I verbalized my disappointment to Gary, but he told me to be patient. "Just wait," he said, smiling, "sometimes it takes a minute." So I waited. And then, oh boy, after my fourth or fifth drag-it hit. I was high. It was a feeling better than I'd even imagined, and immediately I fell in love.

Gary and I smoked that whole bag. The two of us, in four days, smoked an entire bag of weed. I was stoned the whole time. I was ecstatic in my newfound relationship, and my "all or nothing" mentality was in full gear. I remember literally saying to myself, "I love this. I'm going to smoke it every day for the rest of my life." And from that point forward, I started doing exactly that.

From there, life seemed to slow down and speed up all at once. The very next weekend, another friend of mine had a party while his parents were out of town. He asked me to be in charge of getting the booze. I don't know why he singled me out for this mission, but I proved that I was up to the challenge. Eight cases of beer later, arrangements were being made for a little get-together with eight or nine of our friends.

It wasn't supposed to be a big party, but it turned into one-and in trying to keep up with my friends, I drank so much that I blacked out. It was that all-or-nothing mentality again: "If I'm going to have one beer, I may as well have all of them." Although I had been exploring my parents' wet bar on an amateur basis for years, this party took my drinking to a whole new level, and I got wasted. It didn't take much. I don't even remember that night, but after I woke up the next morning, my friends looked at me differently. One of them even said, "Dude, you're a crazy son of a bitch."

Reputations are interesting, aren't they? People's opinion of me seemed to change after that night, and I liked it. It seemed to me that my friends admired me and the absolute reckless way I threw myself into drinking. All of a sudden they thought I was cool-like, really cool. And here's the part I'll never forget: In that moment, my ego kicked in and I remember thinking, "Oh wow! So this is how you get accepted."

I liked the feeling and doubled down on the idea that partying was in my life for good. I committed-if you can believe it—to being the biggest partier at Brighton High School. And, however stupid and misguided my commitment was, I tried to live up to it. I had found what I thought was the secret to popularity in high school, and I wasn't about to let it slip away.

Ever wonder how kids get money for drugs and alcohol when they don't have a job? Surprisingly, it's pretty easy. Kids in general are resourceful, and kids fueled by addiction and a need for acceptance are extraordinarily imaginative. In my case, I would "borrow" liberally from the money roll my dad left in his bedside table. While he slept, I would sneak in and help myself to a $20 bill. Honestly, it could not have been easier. His business was doing well enough that he was none the wiser. And so, between my newfound ability to lie and steal (along with my dad's long-standing trust in me), I was able to get a constant supply of money to support my new habits.

Every Friday, Gary, the same friend who took me to Bear Lake and introduced me to the wonders of weed, met me in the bathroom at Brighton High School and sold me an eighth of an ounce for $15. He wasn't what you would call a "big" drug dealer-he only had enough to supply his buddies. Standing at the urinal, I'd pass him the cash (courtesy of my unsuspecting dad), and he'd slip me the marijuana, which I tucked right into the front of my pants where no teacher would dare inspect. Then we'd both exit the bathroom. Easy stuff, nothing to it. For the rest of the day, I would stroll the halls feeling like a bad-ass and thinking to myself, "Man, I've got pot on me."

The rush of adrenaline that comes with breaking rules can be addictive. I got a thrill from going to class, talking to girls and interacting with teachers while knowing all the time that I had something forbidden, even illegal, in my front pocket. I found that I enjoyed feeling like a rebel. I liked being sneaky. I had evolved pretty naturally from a curious little kid sneaking liquor from his parents' wet bar to a deceptive teenager stealing money from his dad and buying illegal drugs.

And beside the thrill I got from breaking the rules, there was the added benefit of knowing that my reputation around the school was blowing up. I had achieved my goal of being known as one of the craziest partiers in the whole school. In fact, from about that point forward, I was known to my friends as "Drunk Todd." I fully embraced this new persona. And why wouldn't I? For the first time in my life, I felt "cool."

The "bravery" I felt after stealing from my dad and breaking the law under the noses of school administrators spilled over into other parts of my life as well. On the basketball court, I mastered the art of "talking trash" and became this skinny, arrogant punk kid who would get in the face of even the fiercest opponent. I developed quite the reputation on the courts.

As time went on, I worked to perpetuate this reputation not only because it made me feel superior to my peers but because I could tell that it pleased my dad. He liked my newfound sense of confidence. Of course, he had no idea that it was fueled by drugs and alcohol and the false sense of self-importance they gave me. And for my part, I knew that it felt good to make my dad happy.

The balancing act continued throughout my freshman year. I was still obsessively practicing basketball every day. I set silly, meaningless goals for myself. For example, I decided that I had to master the art of dribbling left-handed, so I'd practice for an hour dribbling with my left hand and only my left hand. Over and over the ball would bounce, until it felt like my arm was going to fall off. Although I was technically on the team, I still wasn't getting much playing time. The lack of playing time was embarrassing, so I became determined to make the coach notice my efforts. Throughout the season, I would come home after team practice and take my ball outside to practice some more. For me, there simply weren't enough minutes in the day for basketball. During the summer, I stayed fixated on the next season and getting more time on the court. I doubled my practice hours, and my dad, seeing my dedication, sent me to a couple of basketball camps. Again, I was all in. It was all or nothing for me.

Sometimes a little luck can come in handy. My luck came in the form of genetics. Between my freshman year and my sophomore year I grew 8 inches. Yes, you read that right-8 inches. I ate so much that McDonald's should have sponsored me that year. I grew so fast that I couldn't seem to eat enough to feel full. I was hungry all the time! In an average midday meal I would devour two Big Macs, an apple turnover, a 20-piece chicken nuggets box, two large fries, and a chocolate shake. Amazingly enough, after all of that, I'd still be hungry. I remember laying in my bed in agony from the growing pains. I went from 12th man on the team my freshman year to starting point guard my sophomore year. In fact, in my little world of basketball, I had a phenomenal sophomore year. I lead the team in every category: steals, free throw percentage, scoring. I played some JV and some varsity that season, and we ended up winning the state championship. I won't pretend that it was all my effort, but I was proud to be part of that team and all that we accomplished.

During the last practice of my sophomore year, I had an injury that could have derailed my plans-but instead it ended up helping my game. I was going up for a shot when somebody grabbed both the ball and my finger at the same time, violently breaking a finger on my dominant hand, which required surgery and four pins. I wouldn't be kept down, though. During the two months I was recovering, I didn't slow my practicing at all, but I used my non-dominant hand only. I'd even jump in for pickup games and play left-handed. I was determined to play just as well with my left hand as with my right, and in the end, my game improved dramatically.

Life kept getting better and better. As a junior in high school, I scored 33 points in a single game. Think of that—I was 16 years old and dominating on a varsity high school team, where I was competing against seniors. Thanks to my finger injury and hours of left-handed practice, I could go left or right and use either hand, and my playing finally captured the attention of both my coach and my teammates. Even my dad was constantly building me up. 'This is the year," he'd say. 'This is the year you're gonna get a college scholarship, and you're gonna do great things with your life."

And he was right. I still had a year of high school left, and, exactly as Dad had predicted, colleges began approaching me. I loved the attention. After years of hard work and near anonymity on the court, it felt good to be noticed and praised.

Aside from my dad, Coach Josh Bingham's attention and praise meant the most to me. Coach commented once during practice, "You got more moves than a can of worms, Sly." I clung to that compliment like my life depended on it. And just like that, my teammates, my friends, and even my teachers started using that nickname: Sly Dog. I felt accepted and valued. I never wanted to disappoint Coach Bingham. He had expectations for me and for the team, and I felt driven to meet those expectations.

Of course, throughout this time, I also kept my commitment to myself to be known as Brighton High's craziest partier. With typical teenage tunnel vision, I couldn't see that my commitment to basketball and my commitment to partying might be at odds with each other. I was arrogant, and I wanted to have my cake and eat it too.

All my attention was devoted exclusively to basketball and partying (not necessarily in that order). The academic aspect of life was not at all a priority. Because of this, I believed on some level that I wasn't very bright. What was the benefit of dedicating time and focus to earn good grades when I wasn't even smart? Besides, basketball was going to be my ticket, both to college and to life outside school.

I did the minimal amount of work necessary to pass my classes and ensure that I would not be kicked off the basketball team for academic reasons. When cheating was an option-whether it was copying assignments or getting the answers to tests from creative sources—I took it.

In short, I felt like I had figured out how to play the game of "high school," and I felt comfortable with my decision to focus on basketball and partying. Looking back, it's fascinating to see how bright and smart I actually was ... when it had to do with something that interested me.

During this time—my sophomore and junior years—my body was at peak physical performance, but other aspects of normal life were wavering. The normal amount of drinking and drugging just wasn't cutting it. I didn't realize it, but my body was building a tolerance to those substances, which resulted in not getting the same high. This was frustrating-so naturally, I upped my usage from drinking and smoking pot mostly on weekends to drinking and smoking pot almost every day.

It wasn't hard to pull off. Both my parents worked, so the house was empty during the day. When the lunch bell rang, I'd race home with a few of my friends, throw back a few shots of whiskey from the wet bar, then return to school. There was even time to get high in the parking lot before going to my afternoon classes.

By the end of my sophomore year, though, no amount of pot could satisfy my growing need to be high. I began experimenting with psychedelic mushrooms, combining them with cough syrup as was the current druggie trend. And then, towards the end of my junior basketball season, a "friend" took me into the bathroom at a party and presented me with a line of coke, saying, "This is for you."

I didn't even hesitate.

Chapter Three
"What Goes Up Must Come Down"

"It just seemed to me, that if you valued a thing, you found ways to keep it from being compromised."

- R.K. Lilley

By the start of my senior year I'd achieved the high school dream. I finally had the reputation, both on and off the court, that I had been striving for all my life. My friends regarded me as both an all-star basketball player and as a wild partier. My teachers thought I was a hardworking, morally upstanding student. My parents saw me as the perfect child, fulfilling their dreams for me in every way. Girls flocked around me. I dated a constant stream of cheerleaders while simultaneously passing my classes, leading my team to state championships, and throwing huge weekend keggers. It was everything I'd ever wanted.

Anyone looking from the outside could easily assume that I had it easy. I had them all fooled. Only I knew that these activities were fueled by ridiculous amounts of drugs and alcohol. Everybody else thought that I had it all—that I was invincible. It was a lot like juggling, but instead of keeping clubs in the air, I was juggling family, girls, grades and sports. I made it look easy-until suddenly it wasn't.

The truth has a way of coming to light. I didn't think that I'd ever really get caught or face negative consequences for my dishonesty. The rules didn't apply to me. And on the off chance I started to feel bad, I'd quickly cover it up with whatever drug I could get my hands on. I believed that I was special-and why wouldn't I? So far, I hadn't had to pay the piper.

Fortunately, it turns out that I was not special at all. The night before senior year basketball tryouts, I was at a family friend's house getting high and doing coke. I wasn't concerned about my performance at tryouts the next day because I was the team captain, and the captains are on the team automatically. Special, right? The whole "tryout" thing was more of a formality for me. And with that in mind, I was going to enjoy a normal weekend filled with illicit substances and poor decisions. This "normal weekend" would turn out to be the start of my downward spiral.

Out of nowhere, a gigantic snowstorm hit while I was partying with my friends. At first, I thought this was a stroke of good luck for me. I called my parents, saying that I didn't feel comfortable driving home in the bad weather. My parents were impressed with my good judgment and mature decision-making skills. In actuality, I saw the snow as a chance to extend the party through the night without having to make up a dumb excuse and sell it to my parents. Also, I was already impaired enough that I didn't like my chances of flying under my parents' radar if I were to go home and face them in person.

Even as jacked up as I was, the lies flowed smoothly. "Mom," I said, doing my best to sound mature, "I'm kind of nervous driving home in this storm." She took the bait and, as predicted, advised that I should spend the night at my friend's house. "Just go to school in the morning after the storm passes," she said. Naturally, after getting the green light to spend the night, I threw whatever caution I had left to the wind and finished the task of getting totally and completely wasted.

Tryouts didn't go well at all. I wish I could have seen inside my coach's mind as he watched me drag myself into tryouts the next day. Hungover and strung out, I practically stumbled onto the court. How could he not have known?

He knew something was wrong because it didn't take long for him to pull me aside and demand to know what the hell was wrong with me. Again, the lies flowed easily and effortlessly. "Sorry, Coach," I said, looking as sincere as I could. "I'm not feeling well today."

And it worked. Just as my parents had believed my lies the night before, the coach bought my lies that day. He'd had no reason before then to doubt me, but I could tell something was bothering him.

Something was bothering me too. Up to that point, I'd never had to make excuses on the basketball court. Even then, I had a hard time seeing how doing drugs might have a negative effect on my playing. All signs flashed "HAZARD," but my mind wasn't having it, so I kept on "runnin' and gunnin.'" Looking back, I clearly see the slippery slope, but at the time, I had no concept of the danger. That day was a perfectly horrible start to a perfectly horrible year.

As the school year and the basketball season progressed, it became increasingly apparent to me that I wasn't as in control as I thought I was. I found that I had built up such a tolerance to the substances that I had to use more and more in order to achieve a feeling of normalcy. In fact, being high didn't even feel good anymore-and the drugs became a necessity to just feel normal. The chains of addiction were getting thicker and thicker. Eventually, without chemicals, my body would no longer function physically without going into withdrawal.

For those of you who haven't felt withdrawal, it's like you're being pulled inside out. By the time I was 19, I had to use drugs or drink every single day in a sad effort to stumble through life. And forget about being able to juggle anything in that state of mind. I was a jumble of mood swings-jumpy, anxious, stressed, irritable and depressed. Unstable is probably the best word to describe my mood at the time. Really deep down, I was scared.

People never really knew which Todd they were going to get, so naturally, I isolated myself more and more. The feelings of worthlessness, which I had managed to stave off using alcohol and drugs, returned.

That mean voice in my head returned, louder this time, telling me over and over again that I was no good, nobody liked me, and I looked funny. I believed it, so the voice moved on to bigger and better lies, telling me that I couldn't do anything unless I was high or drunk, that people didn't like me unless my personality or performance was "enhanced" by drugs or alcohol, and that the only value I had to my friends was as a basketball star and a host of epic parties. Needless to say, I became very depressed.

It's not easy talking about suicide. By this time in my life, I'd heard about a few kids who had killed themselves, so the thought came to me that maybe it was time I ended my life too. The message from the voice in my head that I was broken and not enough was a constant background hum for my whole senior year. During varsity basketball season, I seemed to play more bad games than good ones as I relied more and more heavily on drugs and alcohol to maintain any semblance of feeling normal. Strangely, I still did not equate my declining performance on the court with my increased use of drugs—never a conscious thought that drugs might be connected to anything negative. And the hazard lights were getting bigger and brighter.

Life has a way of keeping you honest, doesn't it? I remember one particularly revealing game against Skyline, a neighboring team. The game was important because Skyline featured some big-name players, and my team, Brighton, was ranked No. 1 in the state. It was a high-profile event, and the place was filled to capacity. I had partied heavily the night before and was even high that afternoon before the game.

In a crucial moment near the end of the first half, I positioned myself wide open at the end of the court. My teammate threw me the ball, and I was all alone with a glorious opportunity to score. In my mind, I was right under the basket. I turned around, took my two steps to lay it up … and found I was at the top of the foul line, nowhere near the basket. I threw the ball and completely missed the hoop.

I heard the entire Skyline crowd screaming, "Nice shot!" They were in hysterics, laughing and jeering-and it didn't let up the entire night. Of course, my own inner voice joined right in, saying, "How does the team captain miss that shot? You didn't even hit the rim. See, you really are a joke." My coach was livid, throwing his arms up and swearing. He immediately yanked me out of the game. My heart felt like it was going to pound its way right out of my chest. I was devastated.

Up until this point, I had been showing up at most practices high (not that my coaches knew) but still playing the games clean, for the most part. I thought I had my coaches fooled. After the Skyline game, though, my coaches were all over me, demanding to know what was responsible for my declining performance. My coaches could see that something was wrong-but they didn't know what it was.

At the same time, my own awareness was so low that I still had no clue that the drug use was affecting my life and compromising my dreams. With my level of insight as low as it was, I thought that the problem was all me and the fact that I simply wasn't good enough. This feeling of inadequacy acted like a sledgehammer, and the spike of depression drove me deeper into the arms of the substances that helped me numb the pain. But the drugs or alcohol only lasted so long, and eventually, suicidal thoughts became a regular part of my day.

Somehow, even despite my impaired performance as team captain, Brighton's basketball team made it to the state competition that year. During the state final game, as if by a miracle, everything seemed to come together for me. I was mentally ready for a fight and felt fueled by my all-or-nothing approach. My dad and my coach delivered some amazing pep talks, and I played the game of my life. We demolished the other team.

I was on top of the world, and nobody could knock me down. Reporters wanted to interview me, my coaches and teammates praised me, and the crowd chanted my name over and over. It was like a dream come true.

After the game, like any good addict, I celebrated with drugs. That night, I snorted an 8 ball of cocaine and guzzled beer like there was no tomorrow. A week after that game, I was offered a full-ride basketball scholarship to a local community college. I had achieved my goal (and my dad's goal for me) and decided to devote the final month and a half of my senior year to partying like never before.

Right after graduation, a friend of mine threw a party for the whole senior class. Remember, I had a carefully cultivated reputation of being the wildest partier in the school, so when the beer bong was pulled out, I was all over it. We didn't even come up with a clever or sophisticated drinking game where you had to take a drink if you answered a trivia question wrong or anything like that; we merely went around in a circle and each guy tried to drink more than the guy before him.

I was at the end of the circle. After watching a few of my friends, I thought, 'These guys are lightweights. I'm going to blow them all away." I knew exactly what to do in order to keep my reputation untouchable. When the bong got to me, I poured in a fifth of vodka.

Some in the crowd knew that was a huge amount of alcohol to ingest and were telling me not to go through with it. But I had a reputation to keep up and so, without hesitation, I poured the alcohol down my throat. It took all of three seconds-and this was after I'd already consumed a fair amount of alcohol while awaiting my turn with the bong. Although I was tall, I only weighed 145 pounds, and that fifth of vodka alone would have put my blood alcohol level at .51 (a lethal level is .42).

It took less than five seconds to ingest enough alcohol to kill myself. The last thing I remember was some dude saying, "You're toast."

I woke up 24 hours later, slumped next to a toilet in my friends' parents' bathroom. From the looks of it, I was covered in blood from my head to my toes. I could barely move, and when I did, my whole body screamed in defiance. Death would have felt better.

I couldn't speak at that point, but my friends told me that I'd been puking blood all night and all day. As teenagers, they hadn't known what to do for me and didn't dare call my parents (I don't blame them), so they faithfully kept watch over me until I was ready to go home.

Honestly, I don't remember much of that, but I do remember that my parents were frantic and had the police out looking for me. When I stumbled into the house, they were both hugely relieved and unbelievably angry at the same time, especially when they found out what had happened.

The crazy thing was, I still didn't understand how out of control my behavior was. I had almost died from alcohol poisoning. I should have been dead. You'd think that would have been enough to stop me from continuing to spiral downward, but it wasn't.

The voice inside my head had gotten so loud and convincing that I began not to care about the possibility of death. Even when I was drinking to oblivion or snorting copious amounts of cocaine, I would actually think, "I don't care if I die. I really don't."

Anyone looking at me from the outside would have thought I had it all—that I was the craziest son of a bitch you'd ever seen. But it was all an act. Fake. It was all about me being insecure and overcompensating in order to be liked by others. I wanted to be validated, and I thought that in order to get that acceptance, I had to keep up the act of being the crazy guy, even though I hated everything about my life.

I partied away the summer, and when fall came I started attending classes at Utah Valley Community College. Everything was positioned to transition seamlessly into my career as a college basketball star. Everything but me, that is. I was a hot mess, and it turned out that my college coach had less patience with me than my high school coaches. It didn't take long before he took action.

Two weeks into practices, the coach pulled me into his office. I knew I was in trouble, and I was ready with the normal laundry list of excuses that I typically used to dodge consequences. But this time it didn't work. The coach looked at me in disgust and stopped me short, saying, "I don't have time to screw around. You're not the player I thought you were." He went on to say that there were other kids who had walked onto the team that were playing harder and better than I was playing. And then came the death knell. Without any hesitation he bluntly said that they had already decided to take away my scholarship and award it to someone else.

I was in shock, but I wasn't beat yet. I had one more card to play. Falling to my knees and with tears streaming down my face, I begged him to reconsider. I promised him everything I could think of to change his mind. Nothing would convince him. He had seen all he needed to see in those two weeks of practices; I was not the player he wanted.

Panic. That was my first emotion. Not grief, not sadness, not anger. It was panic. How was I going to tell my dad? I knew that in a way, my dad was living his dreams through me. He loved sports and he loved me for excelling at them. How was I going to tell him that I had blown it? Ultimately, I couldn't tell him.

Like the coward I was, I went home and broke the news to my mom, knowing that she would coddle me and reassure me that everything would turn out OK. And then I left it to her to break the news to my dad. To this day, I don't have a clear recollection of how my dad reacted to me after he learned the news. I do remember feeling defeated, and I spent the next few months in a haze of drugs, alcohol, depression and self-pity. I had no value. Life had no purpose. And the hopeless feeling was never-ending.

This was an all-time low for me, and the longer it went, the more it made sense that I should just die already. I felt like the ultimate failure—I had worked so hard and so long to achieve my dream, and right as it was in the palm of my hand, I blew it up.

There was nobody to blame but myself, but of course I looked everywhere and found plenty to accuse. Coaches, friends, parents, basketball—nothing was safe from my incriminating finger! I could probably have found a way to blame cartoons or even the pizza delivery driver if I really put my mind to it. I was the ultimate victim.

Hindsight is 20/20. Now I can look back and see the truth: that at the end of the day I was not actually a victim of anyone or anything. It was really quite simple—I loved drugs and alcohol more than I loved anything else, including basketball. But at the time, I still wasn't able to admit to myself that I valued being high over everything else in life. As far as I had fallen, I still had further to go. Turns out I hadn't hit rock bottom quite yet.

Chapter Four
"Wrecking Ball"

"Sometimes it takes an overwhelming breakdown to have an undeniable breakthrough."

- Unknown

Everyone needs a purpose in life. Even after losing my basketball scholarship, I continued looking for my purpose where I had always found it before: in sports. I walked on and tried out for a few different college teams that fall, but I ended up getting cut from every one of them. Anger, hurt, frustration and humiliation seemed to cover me like a cold mist—I couldn't shake it. But the worst part about this time of life was being afraid. I was so scared. If sports wasn't my purpose in life anymore-and it was starting to look that way—then what WAS my purpose?

To mask my growing fear and embarrassment, I went back to what I knew. I turned even more completely to drugs and alcohol, and I looked for people with a similar focus that mirrored my own self-destruction. Funny enough, I ended up living in a party house in Orem, Utah, with a bunch of guys from the BYU baseball team. Isn't that odd? Looking back now, the whole thing is surreal. We were a bunch of self-destructive, wannabe athletes who, for one reason or another, were all trying to mask our emotions with chemicals.

This was an angry time of life. As an angry drunk, I would destroy things for no apparent reason at all. Every time I drank, I got violent. Walls were my specialty. I'd punch them and, on occasion, even put my head through them. Furniture wasn't safe either. It wasn't surprising for me to kick, punch, or throw whatever chair that happened to be around. One time, I threw a chair through the front window for no reason at all. A group of us were sitting around partying—no fighting, no argument—nothing exciting going on at all until I blew up and threw a chair through a huge plate glass window. Inside, I felt like a pressure cooker with the lid strapped tight. Eventually the cooker explodes unless the steam is released-but for me, it wasn't heat; it was hurt. It was sadness. And after destroying walls or furniture or whatever had been in my way, I would cry like a little boy.

Nothing mattered to me-literally nothing. My life was ruined, and my living conditions began to mirror the condition of my soul. Even under the best of circumstances, college-age young men are not known for their housekeeping skills. We lived in complete squalor. If I needed to urinate, I walked over to the corner of whatever room I happened to be in and just peed. My roommates did the same. The stench was powerful, but it wasn't enough to make me care or motivate any change to my behaviors.

Our living room featured a beautiful brick fireplace surrounded by more decorative brick. It should have been the focal point of the room, but instead it served as a target for our anger. After drinking beer, we would chuck the bottles against the brick and watch the glass shatter all over the floor. We accumulated quite a heap of broken glass against that fireplace. It collected for months, and I honestly don't know how our feet weren't cut to ribbons as we stumbled drunkenly through the house.

I don't remember how long I'd been living this way, but I know that it was on a Thursday when the reality hit that, for me, basketball was over.

There was no more daydreaming about playing-my chance was gone. My validation was gone. My identity and purpose: gone. I'll never forget sipping on a bottle of Jack Daniels and saying to myself out loud, "I'm done."

As if on cue, the voice inside my head started screaming the same lies it had told me for years. "You're pathetic-kill yourself." Something inside me flipped and I went to an even darker place in my mind. Alone, living in squalor, and finally recognizing that my dreams were dead, I said to myself, "I'm killing myself. It's over. What's the point?" And then, after years of just thinking about suicide, I actually began making a plan to end my life.

There wasn't much to it, really. The plan was simple. After finishing my bartending shift that weekend (not the smartest career choice for an alcoholic but certainly a convenient one), I'd drive to my parents' house in Salt Lake City. I knew my dad had a shotgun, and I knew where he kept it. I planned to do it under the old juniper tree in the backyard, completely hidden from view under its huge branches. If I couldn't reach the trigger, I would use one of the tree branches to pull it and blow my head off.

The juniper tree was somewhat of a sacred place for me as a child. It was a private location to go if I had a bad day at school, if I was sad, or even if I was happy. I knew that I could crawl under its protective branches and be alone with my feelings. The tree was also the place where, as a child doing my Saturday chores, I threw the dog poop. I was supposed to put the excrement in a bag and place it in the trash can, but that had seemed too time-consuming. Anxious as I was to finish my chores and start practicing basketball, I would throw the waste into the corner behind the giant tree. Now, as I planned my suicide, I appreciated the irony: I would now be the piece of shit that would magically disappear in the juniper tree.

As was typical of my complete self-absorption at that time, I didn't wonder how my death would affect my family. I didn't even wonder how long it would take for someone to find me. There was zero thought to who was likely to find me or how the discovery was likely to impact them. I could only think about how awful I felt and how exhausted I was. At this point, I longed for any relief from feeling so sad and alone. I was done feeling like a failure-feeling like I wasn't good enough, feeling like there was nothing for me in this life. I was done with all of it and wanted out.

That was on a Thursday afternoon. Friday came and my suicide plan was still rock-solid in my mind. For lunch that day, I decided to stop at the cafeteria at Utah Valley Community College. I was enrolled earlier in the semester, but since I had dropped all my classes, it was really just a place to hang.

I found my buddies at their usual table in the cafeteria and joined them there. Also at the table were two LOS girls who would sometimes sit with us. Why they chose to sit with us was a mystery to me-because, frankly, I behaved like an ass around them. I knew they were religious, and since I had grown up with a father who was very vocal about his opposition to the LOS Church, I had a never-ending stream of insults to hurl at them.

I'd say things like, "Your church is a joke" or "Why don't you do some-thing useful with your tithing money, like give it to the homeless or some-thing?" I'd even go after Joseph Smith, saying things like, "The guy who started your church was a gold-digger and he used a rock to find gold plates that he wouldn't let anyone see."

Of course, these weren't really my views since I knew next to nothing about the doctrine of the LOS Church—I was used to parroting insults I heard from my dad say over the years in the hopes that I would offend these two girls. And still these two girls continued to sit with me and my crude, obnoxious friends. They would listen to my rants and smile, letting the vile remarks roll off their backs. To this day, I don't know why they continued to sit with us, but thank God they did.

Other than knowing it was going to be my last day alive, this particular Friday was pretty standard. My buddies were casually discussing whatever was going on in their lives as I sat there, half-listening to the conversations going on around me. The talking turned into a background hum while I reviewed my suicide plan over and over in my mind. This idea that finally allowed an escape somehow had me feeling lighter, and the bully inside my mind latched on to this mood, reminding me that the end couldn't come fast enough.

In the periphery of my consciousness, I heard one of the two LOS girls mention something about "fasting and prayer." My attention was caught by that word I'd never heard before: fasting. What the hell? That unfamiliar word just hit me like a gigantic gong of a bell. I felt like the word was important and wondered what it meant.

Of course, I didn't dare ask the girls about it in front of my buddies, so I had to get them alone. When the two left, I followed as inconspicuously as possible. Stopping them in the hallway, I said, "Hey, were you guys just talking about fasting and prayer? What is that?" They looked at me, skeptical. I could tell that they were suspicious of my interest-and they had every right to be, given my past behavior. "Why?" one of them asked. "Are you just going to rip on us?" I answered quickly, "No, I'm serious. I really want to know."

The girls seemed to relax a little and gave me a quick summation. They explained that, once a month, Mormons decide on a purpose or a question they need help with. Starting with a prayer, they then go a full 24 hours without eating or drinking anything. Then they end with a prayer.

I was confused. Since I had no religious background, this made no sense. "What's the point of all that?" I asked them. I'll never forget what happened next. One of the girls looked me dead in the eyes, pointed her finger right in my face, and said, "You do that when you want help from God." Her words were like a hammer blow right between the eyes. That's how it felt.

Because of my upbringing, I didn't believe there was a God, but I also didn't believe there wasn't one. To be honest, I really hadn't put much thought into whether a God existed or not. But at that moment, the thought came to me: "Is there a God, and will He help me?"

Could it really be as simple as not eating or drinking for a day? And if there really was a God, would He help someone like me? So much was going through my head. I thanked the girls (which was probably another shock to them) and walked away. The possibility felt like a hint of hope, and I remember thinking, "I'm going to try this."

Chapter Five
"Seven Words"

"Being vulnerable is the only way to allow your heart to feel true pleasure."

- Bob Marley

I didn't go to my parents' house that night to end my life under the giant tree as I had planned. I didn't even go to my bartending job. For whatever reason, I just decided to stay in Orem that day. Maybe somewhere deep down inside, I knew that getting anywhere near that shotgun was a bad idea. Maybe, deep, deep down inside, I hoped that this "fasting and prayer" thing might be a way out of my miserable life that didn't involve dying.

My conversation with the LOS girls had taken place on a Friday afternoon, and although I didn't go up to Salt Lake as I had planned, I did follow my normal weekend pattern and got wasted that night. Saturday morning came, and it was the same as all the other hangover Saturday mornings I was groggy, depressed, miserable, and sick. But this time I did something different. This Saturday morning I skipped the self-flagellation that normally followed an evening of drinking and decided to act on what I had heard the previous day. I was going to fast and pray.

The girls from the cafeteria said that I needed to start my fast with a prayer. My family wasn't religious, so praying was completely unfamiliar to me. And praying in a party house full of non-religious BYU baseball players seemed even more out of place-like ordering a big steak at a vegetarian party.

I didn't want any of my roommates to know what I was doing, so I went into a teeny-tiny coat closet in the front hall and got down on my knees. I'm 6-foot-3, so folding myself into that tiny space was not easy. I had coats and jackets brushing my head and a stinky collection of athletic shoes underneath me, but somehow I knew that praying had to be done on my knees, so I sucked it up.

I've never been a talker, so my first prayer wasn't lengthy; in fact, it was quite the opposite. My prayer consisted of only seven words altogether: "God, if you're there, I need help."

I had no idea what to do after saying those seven words. So, after a minute, I listened to make sure none of my roommates were around, then stepped out of the closet. The next step was the fasting part, so I began the 24 hours of not eating or drinking.

In typical human fashion, as soon as I decided that I wouldn't eat or drink, suddenly food and drink were the only things I could think about. My stomach growled and my mouth suddenly felt as though I had been crawling through the desert for weeks without liquid.

And in my case, fasting had an added component-for the first time since smoking weed with my buddy at Bear Lake, I was determined to go a full day without ingesting any mind-altering substance. Yes, you read that right. I had been so consistent in substance abuse that it had been YEARS since going more than a couple of hours without using some type of drug.

My first attempt at a 24-hour fast fell short by about 20 hours. The fast started around 9 Saturday morning and stopped by 1 o'clock that afternoon. Altogether I had lasted a full four hours, and it felt like an eternity. I was legitimately going through withdrawals; not just from food and water but also from the chemicals that had sustained me daily for several years. By the third hour, I was physically hurting, and by the fourth hour, I was done.

The LOS girls had said to end the fast with a prayer, so that's what I did. Going back into that same tiny closet, I got down on my knees and said, "God, if you're there, I just did this fast. I need help." Then I waited for God to show up. In my naivete, I actually believed that if God really did exist, He would show Himself to me. So I sat in that little coat closet for a few minutes and waited for God to appear.

Nothing happened, so I repeated myself, this time in a slightly challenging tone: "God, if you're there, show yourself." Again, I waited a few minutes, and again, nothing happened. "Well," I thought, "that was a huge waste of my time." I stood up, walked out of the room and got hammered.

For the next month, I still considered driving to Salt Lake to use my dad's shotgun and end it all, but for some reason I didn't. My hesitation was in no way related to my attempt at fasting; in my mind, that had been an unmitigated failure. Looking back, I don't know why I didn't go to the juniper tree—I just didn't. Instead, I spent the month drinking like a fish and using all the usual drugs. The siren call of the shotgun had, for the moment at least, quieted.

Chapter Six
"Rich"

"Drugs take you to hell ... disguised as heaven"

- Author Unknown

The month that followed was not special. I didn't return to the little coat closet to fast or pray again, but I did continue to cover up my sadness with drugs and alcohol. I also continued to work, albeit sporadically, as a bartender-which meant I had a lot of time on my hands. Extra time isn't necessarily a good thing, especially when someone is depressed. For me it allowed for an endless back-and-forth debate as to whether my life was worth living.

The pro-living side must have held its own, though, because there I was-a month after the unsuccessful fast-still breathing. That's where I was in life—existing unhappily alive in a rundown, unkempt, trash-filled party house-when the phone rang.

The caller was a friend from high school named Rich. We'd played basketball together, and since then, he had gone on a two-year LOS mission, come home, and gotten married. We hadn't stayed in touch at all since high school. He was on a totally different life track than I was at that point, so I was very surprised to hear from him.

In fact, when he identified himself at the beginning of our conversation, it took me a minute to remember him. To make it even more remarkable, this was before social media, texting, or even cell phones. To this day I don't know how he tracked me down-but somehow, Rich had found out where I was living and then gotten his hands on the party house's phone number.

None of my roommates were particularly social, and the phone ringing was a rare enough event that, when it rang that day, I remember thinking, "Who's calling here?"

Our conversation—once I was able to place who the caller was-started off with the usual niceties about where we were living and what we were up to. Of course, in my case, I glossed over the fact that I was living in a dump and getting wasted as often as I could. "I'm in Orem right now" was my answer when he asked where I was. Rich said he was in Orem too and would like to see me. In fact, not only did he want to see me, he wanted to see me that very same day. With that, the phone call went from strange to even stranger. I couldn't figure out why my old high school friend whom I hadn't seen in years was trying to set up a time to meet. But he had piqued my curiosity, and I didn't have anything better to do, so I took down his address and agreed to meet him later that day at his apartment.

The closer it got to our arranged meeting time, the more apprehensive and awkward I felt. Why had I agreed to this? Still, for some reason, I went and soon found myself knocking on Rich's door. He didn't look much different than I remembered—maybe a little rounder in the face but overall the same Rich I had played ball with years earlier.

Looking at his expression, I sensed that this was not going to be an ordinary reunion between old buddies. He looked serious, which was bizarre because I remembered Rich as a real goofball. You know the guy that is always messing around, smiling at anything and having fun all the time? That was Rich. The first words out of my mouth were, "Is everything OK?" He said, "Oh, everything is good! Come on in." With that, my tension eased a little.

I went in and sat down while we chatted about what had been going on the past few years in our lives. Of course, I was very vague and quick with my summation. I tried to talk more about him and his life, attempting to gloss over the sorry state of my own, but Rich didn't seem interested in talking about himself. He seemed more interested in talking about me-as if he had a very specific purpose in mind for this meeting.

It is very uncomfortable hearing good things said about you when you have low self-esteem. Often, you can identify people who are struggling with self-esteem just by observing how they take a compliment. For example, when you tell someone that their hair looks nice and they say anything other than "thank you," that person is likely working through low self-esteem issues. It was no different with me.

Quite suddenly during our conversation, Rich began peppering me with really nice statements. "Todd, you're going to help so many people in this world." He continued, "Todd, you're going to work with the youth and you're going to make a huge difference in this world." I had no idea what he was talking about.

In fact, I wasn't actually hearing him. You know when someone is talking to you and you find yourself not actually listening because there is a voice in your own head that's louder than the voice they're speaking with? That is what was happening to me while Rich was talking. As he spoke, I kept hearing my own negative voice inside my head. (I now call that voice "the bully," but back then I didn't have a name for it—I just listened to it yammering away inside my head like that one annoying guy who never shuts up.) "Geez," the bully said. "Rich obviously doesn't know me very well.

I'm a drug addict. I'm selfish. I lie, I cheat, I steal, I manipulate." And yet Rich continued saying nice things about me. This type of talk was so foreign to me that I found myself wondering if I was being punked–if this was all part of an elaborate prank.

Rich went on like this for a very uncomfortable five minutes until finally I stopped him. "Dude," I said, "I don't know why you're saying this, but you have no idea how bad my life is right now. I'm miserable. My life is a mess and I have no idea what you're talking about." At this point, the feeling in the room became more serious but he just looked at me in silence. Growing impatient, I asked him, "Where is this even coming from and why did you call me here?"

Rich looked relieved, as if my question was what he had been waiting for. "Todd," he said, "I didn't go to work today because I needed to share a message with you." This surprised me, and I asked him again if everything was OK. He assured me that things were good, but I could tell that he was having difficulty getting around to what he really wanted to say. Finally, after some more awkward silence, he took a deep breath and, looking me right in the eye, said, "Todd, the Lord came to me last night and told me that we needed you on our side today."

Out of that whole astounding sentence, the word "today" was the one that stood out to me. That single word made Rich's whole utterance feel urgent. Gradually, though, the other parts of Rich's statement began to sink in too. I remembered the failed fast, and particularly the prayer. Was God really there? Had he really spoken to Rich about me? My head was spinning. Part of me was waiting for Rich to deliver the punchline of this grand joke, but no punchline ever came.

At the time, I could not have explained the feeling that came over me as I sat there on Rich's couch. Knowing what I know now, I can identify the feeling as God's love. It was an overwhelming warmth of love and peace washing over me like a wave. It was like nothing I'd ever felt before-almost like when you're wading in the ocean and a wave washes up and covers your whole body, knocking you backwards. Because the feeling was so intense and so completely new, I was a little bit scared. What was going on? I was completely flooded and so was Rich. We were both in tears as we sat there, just feeling the peace and joy that filled his little apartment.

Deja vu is a feeling of recollection or familiarity—the feeling that whatever you're experiencing at that moment, you have experienced that thing before. What happened to me that day in Orem was more than deja vu. The experience wasn't just familiar—I KNEW that it was an answer. I can't explain it, but as everything was happening, my mind went back to that moment in the coat closet when I was on my knees beginning my fast. I recalled it perfectly: the little closet, the dirty clothes all around me, and my plea to God. With tears in my eyes, I told Rich that I'd fasted about a month ago asking God for help. I'll never forget Rich's response. Without hesitation, he said, "This - is - your - help." Again, the floodgates opened and we both felt what I can only describe as pure acceptance and love. We just sat there in silence trying our best to emotionally absorb what was happening. I don't know how long we sat there or how the next part of the conversation started, but I remember asking Rich, "Now what?"

Chapter Seven
"Just Show Up"

"If You're Honest You'll Never Relapse"

- Todd Sylvester

A lot can happen in a day. My Saturday had started with a massive hangover coupled with the usual feeling of hopelessness. I had nowhere to be, nobody to be with, and no purpose to my life. My existence had no meaning. I felt like I was nothing.

But now, in just a few short hours, everything had changed. I was something. I was important. God actually existed and cared about me enough to answer my call for help. The change was so drastic that I wasn't sure how to cope, and I reverted to my narrative of what a big mess I was. I tried to convince Rich how broken I was. I still believed that I was not worth anything or had anything of value to give. The shame of what my life had become started falling on me like a cold, familiar rain, and the bully inside my head was louder than ever. But Rich wouldn't accept my attempts to dismiss myself.

Shame is an interesting thing. It seems to just stick to you until it covers your whole body and your identity. After so many years of carrying shame around, I was a pro at it. Everything that was happening in Rich's small apartment was going directly against what I'd created as my identity.

This was a real dilemma.

My friend seemed to sense what I was going through and said, "You need to go see your bishop." Now, remember, I was not LOS. I wasn't anything, really. I had no religious education or foundation at all. I had just said my first prayer EVER about a month prior to this.

So naturally, my reaction to Rich's proclamation that I needed to see my bishop was this: "I don't think I have one." Rich didn't miss a beat. "Yes, you do," he said. "You just don't know it."

For the next hour, Rich made phone call after phone call trying to determine who my LOS bishop would be. He was tenacious. I didn't know it then, but LOS bishops are assigned to certain geographic areas. Rich wisely thought that it would be best to connect me with the bishop assigned to my parents' home in Salt Lake City rather than the bishop who would have been assigned to the party house in Orem.

Committing to do something uncomfortable is ... well, uncomfortable. After Rich had spent an hour on the phone, he finally came back to me with news. "I got you an appointment tomorrow with your bishop," he said. "You'd better show up."

I didn't understand why I had to tell yet ANOTHER person how bad my life was and asked Rich why I had to meet with this guy. What was so important about meeting with this one particular man? Rich said I needed to tell the bishop everything I had been doing. "Everything?" I asked. "I can't do that." Immediately my brain started thinking myself out of the meeting.

I knew Rich wouldn't let me use the "I don't have time" excuse, so my mind skipped straight to excuses like "This guy doesn't even know me. He wouldn't understand." Or "What does it even matter that I tell anyone what I've done? This is about me, not him." But Rich stopped me cold by getting right in my face and saying, "You better just show up. Oo I have your word?"

I found my mind reviewing the new feelings I'd had in the last hour with Rich—that feeling that maybe God did know who I was after all, and I heard myself say, "OK, I'll do it."

I didn't know what to expect as I drove to the meeting. The battle in my head was raging. One side was reminding me how crazy this was and kept asking why I was even going. The other side kept recalling the experience I had had the day before. I had felt something wonderful and I couldn't deny that, so on I went. The address Rich gave me led to an LOS church. If you've ever seen an LOS church-anywhere in the world—you'll be able to imagine what this church looked like: a big red brick building complete with a steeple and a sign outside reading "Visitors welcome." There was one lone car-an old red Buick—parked outside the church. The rest of the parking lot was deserted.

I'd never been to a church, but for some reason I expected that there'd be a lot of cars and people milling around. But that night, it was just the red Buick waiting for me. My heart felt like it was going to explode as I pulled into the parking lot, so I did the logical thing and started to drive away.

I was well on my way out of that parking lot when my mind was filled with the image of Rich asking, "Oo I have your word?" The sound of his voice bounced around in my head until I couldn't take it anymore. I turned the car around and headed back into the parking lot, parking next to the red Buick.

"I'll give him five minutes," I said to myself. "I'll let this guy tell me what he needs to tell me and then I'm out of there." I walked into the building and there he was waiting for me: the bishop. He didn't look special-just a guy in his late 40s or early 50s, average height, and balding. He also had a really big smile-seriously, it was a big, big smile. And he kept that smile focused on me as he led me to his office and invited me to sit down, telling me that his name was Bishop Taylor.

I felt welcome, but it was still awkward. How was this going to start? What was I even supposed to tell him? As we sat down across from each other, my mind was starting to buzz. I looked at the clock, which read 6:04. "Five minutes," I thought to myself.

Connection could very well be the opposite of addiction. In other words, addicts typically cut themselves off from society or personal ties. This happens in a couple of ways. First, there's the illegal aspect and eventually, people getting caught. The resulting charges lead to jail time or being labeled a criminal, and either one of those results in being outside social norms. Isolation.

I was fortunate enough to never have any legal consequences, but that didn't keep me from disconnecting from my family and friends. Think about it-why would I want to be around anyone when I believed I wasn't worth being around?

That phrase, "Connection is the opposite of addiction," explains in a way what happened as I sat across from Bishop Taylor that night. "So, tell me what's up," he said. And then he sat back in his chair and didn't say another word. He patiently waited for me to talk. At first, I fumbled around trying to express myself. "I'm not sure why I'm supposed to be here," I finally said. "I was just told to come and talk to you." This was good; I was talking.

After that initial sentence, when Bishop Taylor still didn't say anything, I figured that it would be good for him to know why this appointment had been made, so I started telling him the story of what had happened between Rich and me the day before. Bishop Taylor quietly listened. He didn't interrupt; he didn't give advice or direction. He simply listened.

After I told him about my experience with Rich the day before, I began talking about everything that had led up to that point, and I mean everything. I unloaded on this dude for three hours. I didn't only tell him about my partying; I told him about the lying, the cheating, the stealing, and the stuff I was doing with girls.

I was living a bad life; I really was. At my core, I was a good person, and people thought I was nice, but I was doing some really horrible things, and I dumped all of it onto this poor guy I had barely met. It felt a lot like throwing up. The vomit is exiting your body whether you like it or not, and it is going to keep coming until it's all out.

That is how I felt once I started talking. Everything was going to come out, and once I got started there was no stopping it. I went into vivid detail, telling Bishop Taylor things I'd never told anyone. I guess I figured that, hey, I was there, I might as well lay it all on the table.

All throughout the meeting, I kept expecting Bishop Taylor to condemn me as too evil to be on church grounds and demand that I leave the premises immediately, but he never did. He listened. That was probably the most surprising thing about the meeting for me: Bishop Taylor simply let me talk without judging me.

This was surprising because my own inner dialogue harassed me continually with insults and condemnation. I expected other people would do the same thing if they ever found out how I really behaved when nobody was watching. But this man was not condemning at all. He seemed to genuinely care about me, and just as surprising, he seemed happy that I was there.

When I was done talking, more than three hours after I had started, I felt relief. Just as you always feel better when you're done throwing up, I felt so much better after letting all my thoughts and emotions out. But alongside my feeling of relief, there was a little bit of apprehension. I had no idea how Bishop Taylor was going to respond to my confession.

I tried to recall what I had heard priests in movies and on TV say. "Go now, my son, and sin no more?" Would I be required to do some type of penitent act? Maybe say a few Hail Marys or count beads on a rosary? Whatever it was, I was pretty sure that God was going to want some kind of payback for all the wrongs I'd committed.

"There are four things I want you to do," he began. My heart leapt into my throat. Here it comes, I thought. This is where he asks me to go and "sin no more" or some other impossible thing I can't commit to. Bishop Taylor continued, "Do you think you can say one prayer a day like you did when you were in that closet? One simple prayer. Do you think you can do that?"

I was relieved. This was doable. Sure, I could say one prayer a day. I heard myself agreeing to his request while bracing myself for the next request. He reached over and pulled out a set of scriptures, which included the King James Version of the Bible-both the Old and New Testaments-along with a Book of Mormon. The stack of books loomed large in front of me, and I panicked a little, thinking he was going to ask me to read all of them.

"Have you ever read these before?" he asked. "Never," I replied. Bishop Taylor didn't furrow his brow or frown in disappointment. Instead, he asked that I read one verse a day. "I don't care if you don't even understand it; just read one verse every day. Can you do that?" Again, I nodded in agreement, committing to read one random verse of scripture a day. "I can probably do that," I said.

Bishop Taylor smiled and leaned forward as he prepared to make his next request. I caught the body language loud and clear and thought, "Here it comes. He started with the easy stuff. Now comes the thing I won't be able to do." I held my breath, waiting for the bishop's next demand. "I need to meet with you every week for a year," he said earnestly. My reply was immediate. "I can't do that." There was no room for negotiation on my end about this. His request was too much to ask from me. I wondered how he was going to respond, but he only nodded understandingly. "We'll take it a week at a time, but I want to see you for a year ... at least," he said.

As a 21-year-old, the thought of meeting with someone every single week felt like a prison sentence, so Bishop Taylor's willingness to be flexible about the frequency of our meetings was crucial. I had a history of battling inflexible people (mainly authority figures) with my own pigheaded stubbornness. I don't know if Bishop Taylor sensed this about me, but his flexibility made it possible for me to agree to that third request.

Now we had only one more to go. Bishop Taylor seemed to relax. He must have thought that getting me to commit to seeing him for a year would be the most difficult request of the four he planned to make, but he was wrong. I was in no way, shape or form ready for what came out of his mouth next.

Settling back into his chair, Bishop Taylor said, "The fourth thing is that I need you to be honest with me." I was taken aback, confused and reflexively defiant. My criminal, habitually manipulative mind went looking for loopholes. "What do you mean?" I asked. "When we meet," Bishop Taylor said, "I need you to tell me if you drank, if you got high, if you cheated, if you lied, if you did anything with a girl, or if you've looked at pornography." He then continued down the list of all the things I'd been struggling with. Basically, he targeted everything I'd spent the last few hours spilling my guts about. It was a long list.

I opened my mouth to deliver a defensive, smart-aleck reply but instead heard myself saying, "Bishop, I just told you everything, so I can do that." It was done. I had actually pledged myself to fulfil four long-term commitments to some guy I didn't even know who belonged to a religion I wasn't even a part of.

It felt crazy but it also felt right. Committing to do those four things felt like I had finally stumbled onto a paved road after wandering around through thick, prickly sagebrush for years. It felt like more than seeing light at the end of the tunnel. It was more hopeful than that.

Life wasn't going to get better eventually; it already felt better. Like, there was an immediate turning on of lights—not a harsh difference in light and definitely not a bright light, but enough light to make me realize that I'd been living in a very dark place, comparatively speaking. I'd grown used to living in this darkness of misery and hopelessness, but now suddenly someone had turned up the lights and instantly I was more OK than I had been.

It's difficult to explain. Maybe it was awareness that my situation wasn't hopeless, that life could be better than I had believed. I don't know exactly what it was, but I was no longer comfortable being the old Todd—the kid who had awakened earlier that morning hungover, alone and hopeless.

Chapter Eight
"The Lemonade Stand"

" The worst enemy we will ever face in life is the one between our ears"

- Unknown

I don't know what's more surprising: the fact that I actually met with Bishop Taylor every week, or the fact that I continued using drugs and alcohol, even as I was meeting with him.

Or maybe the most surprising thing was that I followed through on my pledge to be completely honest with him. Our weekly meetings went like clockwork. Bishop Taylor would begin, "How was the week, Todd?" and I'd answer, "Got high or drank every day this week, Bishop." It took me eight months of weekly visits to finally be able to look him in the eye and say, "I made it three days without using this week."

I didn't realize it then, but I understand now, that Bishop Taylor's immediate goal wasn't for me to stop using drugs. Ultimately, of course, that was the goal. But at the beginning, the real goal was for me to learn the importance of honesty. Honesty is the most important aspect of recovery, and those weekly meetings with Bishop Taylor taught me how to be honest. In fact, honesty is so paramount that I promise my clients even today that if they are 100 percent honest, they will never use drugs or alcohol again.

Seeing Bishop Taylor also gave me someone to vent to. I needed someone to whom I could complain about how awful my life was and then list the numerous reasons why it was horrible, and I needed that person to agree with me while nodding his head up and down. How was I supposed to stop using drugs when I had every reason to use them?

I laid my excuses in front of the bishop like trophies. I blamed my drinking on my dad. It was his fault for putting so much pressure on me and for only accepting me when I played sports. I even faulted ol' Pops for setting up the basketball court in our yard because if he hadn't done that, I wouldn't have practiced so much and ultimately might not have gotten the scholarship. In my mind, that would have led to me living a normal, drug-free life.

Fascinating, isn't it? The amount of justification I found to excuse my own bad behavior was ludicrous. I had a lot of resentment towards my dad, and I held on to it like a warm blanket fresh out of the dryer. I didn't want to give it up because it allowed me to be a victim, which, conveniently enough, allowed me to avoid accountability for my own actions.

There was also a tug of war going on in my head. The bullying voice that constantly hurled insults at me didn't go away after meeting with Rich and Bishop Taylor. If anything, it got louder. "You are and always will be a loser. You're no good. You can't do it. This is too hard. Nobody likes you."

Those were the old classics, but the bully in my head doubled down and came up with a few new ones. My favorite one sounded something like this: "Bishop Taylor doesn't really want to meet with you. He's only meeting with you because he has to."

Although I didn't want to kill myself anymore, I was still struggling emotionally with depression and feelings of worthlessness. And why wouldn't I be? I still believed I was a victim to a lot of life circumstances that easily justified and even excused my addictive behaviors. In fact, the only real difference behaviorally in my life was the weekly meeting with the bishop.

Even my job was the same. Bartending was really the only trade I knew, and at the time I saw no reason to give up a job I was good at. It's funny now, the justifications I made up to keep a job that readily supplied the very substance I so desperately wanted out of my life.

I was good at bartending, and I made a game out of getting tips. I was almost as skilled at the tip game as I was at basketball. When a customer would come to the bar, I would give him the first drink for free. 'This one's on me," I would say. This clever tactic resulted in the customer thinking not only that I was pretty great, but also that he owed me, which resulted in a bigger tip.

On top of that, I got a share of the tips from the waiters and waitresses working, so I left each night with a good amount of cash. Generally speaking, Utahns have a reputation for being a bit stingy with their money, so I was left with a lot of loose change rather than actual paper money. I didn't mind. Money was money, and the fact that I felt sneaky getting more tips from the customers made up for the fact that most of it was in coins.

Life trudged on and did not seem to be improving much. Looking back, I guess that's not surprising given the fact that I was making very little effort to improve it beyond attending my weekly meetings with Bishop Taylor. I was in a rut. The only thing that was improving was my ability to weasel bigger and bigger tips out of the customers at the bar. By the time my eighth month of meeting with the bishop rolled around, I had a treasure trove of loose change accumulated in my car. Nickels and dimes were strewn about the center console of the car, but I reserved the easily accessible cup holders for quarters.

After months of bartending and squirreling away my tips, I had a lot of quarters—maybe $40 worth. Having 160 or so quarters readily available in my car didn't really mean much to me. I placed more value on people liking me, which is what the tip money represented.

It's fascinating where we find value in life. Some people find it in money, some in athletics, and others in family. I was finding it, at that time in my life, in the fact that people liked me enough to give me loose change out of their pockets. I didn't realize it at the time, but those cup holders full of quarters, which didn't mean much to me monetarily, would later come to be instrumental in changing what I believed my value to be.

The term "Kairos moment" comes from a Greek word used to define a critical or opportune moment. These events can be small or big or anything in between. I had a "Kairos moment" one sunny Saturday morning about eight months after I started meeting with Bishop Taylor. I really had no place to be; I was merely out driving about, enjoying the sunshine. The bully in my brain was in top form, listing for me all of the things that were defective about my life, my appearance, and my personality.

As I drove, wallowing in self-pity, I passed a little girl working a lemonade stand. In the summertime, residential neighborhoods are full of these little entrepreneurs. They set up a card table on a neighborhood street corner and wave homemade signs that say things like "Ice cold lemonade!" That morning alone, I had probably already passed two or three of these lemonade stands, so imagine my surprise when a clear impression came into my mind, saying, "Turn around and give that little girl all the money in your car." Perplexed, I looked back at the little lemonade stand in my rearview mirror getting smaller and smaller. It was almost out of sight before I finally gave in, saying to myself, "Well, this will be kind of cool," before making a U-turn and heading back to her corner.

The little girl had blond hair and blue eyes. I thought she was about nine years old, but guessing the ages of little kids wasn't one of my strong suits, so I may have been wrong. Outfitted with a proper stack of Dixie cups and two pitchers of lemonade, she meant business. I pulled up at the curb next to her and rolled down my window.

Since I had already made up my mind to give her all the money in my car, the price didn't really matter to me, but protocol is protocol, so I smiled and asked, "How much?" "Twenty-five cents," she replied. This was right in line with the going price for a neighborhood lemonade stand, so I nodded and said, "I'll take one". Snapping into action, she smiled and poured me a cup, carefully handing it to me through the open window. I took a sip from the top and set the cup on my dashboard.

"Here goes," I thought to myself, and then said, "OK, hold your hands out like this." I cupped my own two hands together in a bowl shape. She mimicked the shape, holding her own two small hands out. I reached over and dug into my cup holders full of quarters. I scooped up a handful and watched her eyes light up as I held them out to her. This was a lot more than 25 cents! She accepted the first handful and watched in delight as I twisted around to grab more coins. "Hang on, I've got more" I said.

I passed scoop after scoop of quarters out through my car window into her waiting hands. I couldn't help smiling as the coins kept coming and she looked more and more shocked. "Thank you so much!" she said over and over. After the ninth scoop, she piled the coins on the card table and took off in a dead run toward what I assumed was her house. I wondered if she was going to tell her parents that she'd just been given a million dollars.

I had never done anything like this before in my life. I couldn't remember ever giving another person so much joy. Pulling away from the curb, I thought to myself, "That was so cool." But the further I drove, the more I began to feel something that is difficult to explain. Tears formed in my eyes as I kept hearing that little girl saying, 'Thank you so much" over and over. I pictured the quarters overflowing in her little hands, and the amazement of it all kept playing over and over in my mind. I had undoubtedly made that little girl's day ... maybe even her entire month! The tears came slowly at first, so I was able to wipe my eyes and continue driving, but before long the tears were coming faster and I had to pull the car over. I began to bawl.

As the tears flowed, I wondered what was happening to me. My heart began to swell with a feeling that I'd either never felt before or had entirely forgotten. I didn't know what it was exactly, but it didn't matter because it felt good, like a weight was being lifted from my heart.

I don't know how long I was there, sobbing in my parked car. Maybe 5 minutes, maybe 20. The length of time wasn't important. What mattered is that my soul was being cleansed. Is there a word for crying and laughing at the same time? There should be—that's what I was doing as the memory of the little girl's expression of pure happiness played over and over in my head.

It must have looked like I'd lost my mind to anyone watching, but I didn't care. I was happy. Finally, the bullying voice inside my head was silent, and in that moment, I felt ... joy.

Chapter Nine
"All Or Nothing"

"You can't go back and change the beginning, but you can start where you are and change the ending."

- CS Lewis

Habits make the world go round. Well, they make at least 40% of the world go round, anyway. One habit I've been prone to is what some might call an "all or nothing" mentality. I may have picked this up from my mom, who, after 20 years of smoking, decided to give it up cold turkey. One day she simply stopped smoking.

I've read that we repeat 40% of our behaviors on a daily basis purely out of habit, and it's rare to find someone who's self-aware enough to notice their tendency to repeat the same behaviors day after day. Often we need someone else to point it out before it comes into our view.

Let me give an example. Suppose that you drive to work five days a week. It's mundane to the point that there are days that you end up in the parking lot at work and think, "Oh, I'm here already!" Plain old habit got you there, with you putting very little thought or energy into the drive.

Why does this happen? It's because we literally are on "autopilot" for much of our lives. Your brain goes into this robotic, mindless behavior when doing the same activities frequently. And this is all very innate-in other words, we're born with it. Humans use this to help conserve energy that we may need for new situations or circumstances that arise that we don't already have a routine for. Your morning procedure is the same: wake up, turn off the alarm, check your phone, take a shower, get dressed, eat breakfast, etc. You don't really have to think about it—your brain merely directs the body to do what it always does.

Precisely as our behaviors can turn into habit, so can our thinking. I had a well-established pattern of thinking at the time I first encountered the lemonade stand, and it wasn't serving me well. But visiting the lemonade stand started a shift in me. Pulling my car over and releasing all my sadness in the form of "Niagara Falls" from my eyeballs was necessary.

This Kairos moment marked the beginning of my life changing forever. After taking a few moments to make sure I was done bawling my eyes out, I began driving away. Here's where my all-or-nothing mentality kicked in: As I drove off, I remember thinking, "If that girl is there next Saturday, I'm going to give her all my money."

So the next week, and on purpose this time, I made my way toward the corner where the girl and her lemonade stand had been the week before. To my delight, the little girl was there again. She recognized my car pulling up, and as I got closer I could see her eyes were huge and her mouth was forming the words, "Whoa, it's him!"

"I'll take another one," I said after gliding to a stop. She seemed nervous as she filled the cup, but that quickly gave way to glee as I dumped another $15 in quarters into her small hands.

The next week I gave her $20 in one-dollar bills.

The week after that I gave her $30 in quarters.

I was in the process of creating a habit—the habit of driving to the lemonade stand and giving that girl all my tip money. I went every week for 10 weeks-all summer long-and every time I pulled away from the curb, tears would pour down my cheeks. I'd have to pull over and just let it out. I was being purified from the inside out, and in those moments I thought over and over, "I want to be clean. I feel like I matter. I feel like I'm enough." One of my favorite quotes is "The most powerful weapon on earth is the human soul on fire." Going to that lemonade stand and giving to that little girl LIT MY SOUL ON FIRE.

There comes a time when wanting to change life becomes more than words. I'd said the words, "This is my last drink" or "I'm never doing drugs again" plenty of times, but it was only after the lemonade stand that I actually felt like my life was worth changing.

Before that I'd only been able to be sober for very short periods of time, but now I felt clean. It's a lot easier to stay clean from drugs and alcohol when there's less shame in your life. For me, there's a difference between being "sober" and being "clean." People can be sober while experiencing all their usual negative feelings. This is what the common term "white knuckling" means. You'll hear this term utilized when people crave drugs or alcohol but resist the behavior through sheer willpower. It is exhausting, which explains why people "fall off the wagon" over and over.

Being truly clean began when I started living without the constant urge to cover up negative emotions. Notice the word "constant" in the previous sentence. Feeling good about myself didn't happen overnight. It took time.

The feeling I got from visiting the lemonade stand was powerful, but it wasn't there all the time. Rather, it was like trying to hold onto sand: You can take a big scoop, but over time it slowly trickles out of your grasp. Driving away from the lemonade stand (after bawling), I felt invincible. I felt like I was someone—not the person who that bully in my head said I was, but someone good. Someone honest. Someone who cared for others and actually did nice things for other people without expecting something shallow in return.

It was an amazing feeling, but it was temporary. I was staying sober for longer and longer periods of time, but it didn't last. The longer I was away from the lemonade stand, the harder it was to remember that cleansing feeling and my motivation to stay clean wavered.

Growth happens when you do things that are uncomfortable. It had been almost 11 months since I had agreed to Bishop Taylor's four requests. Praying was becoming more and more comfortable, reading the scriptures was becoming more and more bearable, and I hadn't ever missed even one of our weekly meetings.

Even more incredible was that I was being honest-100% honest. I didn't realize it then, but keeping these four pledges that Bishop Taylor had committed me to was helping me create new behaviors—new habits. And my new behaviors were in line with the behaviors of someone who was good, someone who mattered.

Simultaneously, my thinking about myself also began to change. The change was very slow, but it was there. I wasn't listening to the bully in my head telling me that I was worthless, as I had been for years and years. Instead, I began telling myself the exact opposite: that I was a good person. That I was worth something. That I was happy. It wasn't a big dramatic shift, but it was something. And I'd tasted it for long enough that I knew I wanted more.

One day I decided to go to church. The funny thing about this was that Bishop Taylor had never even mentioned church. Through all of those weekly meetings, he had never asked more of me than those original four agreements. I never would have imagined that praying, reading one verse of scripture, meeting with Bishop Taylor and being honest in that meeting would have done anything, but it did. A shift had begun in my life, and now I felt more hope than I'd felt in years. I was looking forward to each Saturday more than I had ever looked forward to anything. Saturday meant that I got to fill that little girl's hands with quarters, and it also meant that my own cup of joy would be filled. My hope was that attending church would help me figure out how to keep my cup fuller for longer than a few days.

That first Sunday, I entered the church building like a lost puppy. I can't remember how I knew what time the first meeting started, but by some miracle, I showed up at the right time. Planting myself in the back corner of the room, I took in the unfamiliar surroundings. The room was big, probably half the size of a basketball court. An organ on the right side of the pulpit area had pipes that stretched from the floor to the ceiling. There was a glossy brown piano to the left of the pulpit, and the pulpit itself was dead center.

But the rows and rows of seats behind the pulpit, facing the congregation, worried me. I later learned that these seats were for the church leaders along with the choir, but on that first Sunday those chairs baffled me. All I could think about was that whoever sat in those seats would be staring straight at me. Luckily, only a few people were sitting in those seats, and I was on the very back row of the chapel. I relaxed a little.

Church definitely was not my normal scene. And like any uncomfortable person in an unfamiliar place, I began scanning the venue to see what I could see. What I found were old people and young people, small families and big families. Single girls my age were … nowhere. "That's OK," I said to myself. "You're not here to hook up."

Continuing the scan of the room, I noticed that everyone seemed to be connected and at ease. They appeared happy, which was odd to me.

Soon, a little girl's frantic movements caught my attention. She was tugging on her mom's dress and pointing at me. In an instant I noticed the girl from the lemonade stand. In semi-shock, I could make out her words—"Mommy, Mommy! That's the guy!" I wanted to pull out my empty pockets and shrug as a joke, but the meeting was about to start, so I smiled and waved politely. As everyone settled down and focused their attention on the speakers, I sat in my chair bewildered at the serendipity of it all. "What are the odds?" I thought.

When the meeting ended, the lemonade girl's mom rushed right up and hugged me. It must have looked to everyone else like she was reuniting with a long-lost family member. With tears in her eyes, she whispered, "Thank you so much for what you have done for my daughter."

I was stunned. There have only been a few moments in my life when I've been able to say exactly how I felt and what I meant—this was one of those moments. My voice choked with tears, I replied, "You have no idea what she has done for me." How could I explain that her little girl had given me the chance to cleanse my soul week after week?

Our embrace ended, and we began talking. Actually, our conversation consisted mostly of the mom talking about how much her daughter thought of me. Apparently she thought I was the greatest guy in the world—not unexpected, given that I had filled her hands with piles of money week after week. But from her initial excitement about the money had stemmed a fondness for me. And from that fondness had grown care and concern for me. And now, at the end of the summer, that little girl saw me as her champion.

The mom went on to explain that her daughter started the lemonade stand to save up for a trampoline, and my lucrative weekly visits had put her well over the top.

As I talked to the mom and her little girl, I felt warm and welcome, as if I was standing in front of a fire on a cold night. As the chapel emptied, we walked to the foyer and continued chatting. The little girl didn't say much, but she didn't need to; her smile and dancing eyes said everything.

After a few minutes of conversing, the mom suddenly looked apprehensive. "We have a favor to ask you," she said. In the past, these words would have filled me with anxiety about how I was about to be inconvenienced, but today was different. Today, I wasn't nervous at all. Somehow, my walls were so far down that I met her question by responding, "Sure, what do you need?"

"On Wednesday, there is a daddy-daughter date, and Lindy wants to know if you would go as her date."

Curious and not wanting to step on any toes, I cautiously asked about Lindy's dad. "We were divorced when she was very young," replied her mom, "and he's not around. She would really like to go with you."

Fifteen minutes earlier, I hadn't even known this little girl's name, so I surprised myself when I instantly said, "Of course I will. That sounds fun." Lindy and her mom beamed at me.

The life of an addict is chaotic. Time almost becomes irrelevant as it's spent in the pursuit of the next fix. Most daily structure flies out the window, much like the chair I threw through the living room window at the height of my addiction. Our motivation switches from family, school and work to drugs, drugs, drugs. We also turn into world-class manipulators and liars. If you don't have what we want, we move on. If you won't give us what we want, we will say or do anything to change your mind. We become more and more selfish as the drugs become more and more important. This leads to burning family bridges and incinerating life opportunities.

I had only to look at myself to see the truth of this. I'd blown a full-ride basketball scholarship because I loved drugs more than basketball. I'd pushed my family further and further away with lies and deception because I loved drugs more than my family. I quit school and half-heartedly kept a part-time gig tending bar because my love of drugs came before my desire to make anything of my life. Probably the scariest of all was that, through all of this, I'd grown used to feeling depressed and hopeless, to the point that I had actually been planning my own death.

But Lindy at the lemonade stand never saw Todd the addict. And neither did her Mom. It's strange now to think that Lindy's mom, Bonnie, had no idea she was asking a drug addict to take her fourth-grader on a church outing.

Wednesday was coming sooner than I wanted, and the closer it got, the more I wanted to back out. Over and over, I questioned why I ever agreed to do this, but when the day arrived, I showed up on Lindy's door-step. I was scared to death and nervous-worse than first-date nervous. I didn't even know this 10-year-old. Come to think of it, I didn't know any 10-year-olds! What would we even talk about?

The church-sponsored "daddy-daughter date" ended up being a picnic held in a nearby canyon. As we drove away from Lindy's house, I tried some small talk, asking Lindy how her recess was that day. Even though I had no clue what I was doing, Lindy looked relaxed and excited about going to the picnic. Mostly, she seemed to be happy that I was there. Not even my awkward and boring questions could knock me off the pedes-tal she had built and placed me on. I found that I liked that feeling.

Chapter Ten
"Pivot"

"Nothing in the world is worth having or worth doing unless it means effort, pain, difficulty... I have never in my life envied a human being who led an easy life."

- Theodore Roosevelt

Driving up the canyon to the picnic should have been relaxing. It wasn't. I was so focused on the map to the picnic site that I was unable to appreciate the beautiful surroundings. The map looked like it had been hand-drawn by someone in a rush, but it was all I had to guide me.

Lindy helped out as much as she could by describing the picnic area and insisting that we were going the right way, but I didn't put much stock in her reassurances-after all, she was 10 years old. Quite like an actual dad, I pretended to listen to her while focusing on the map, and eventually we arrived at our destination.

Like the gentleman I was pretending to be, I opened the door for my date. She smiled and even took my hand while climbing out of the car, and we headed to the gathering. It wasn't quite a sea of fathers with their daughters, but there were enough dad-types for me to feel intimidated. These guys seemed to have their acts together—the exact opposite of how I felt about myself. Similar to when I entered the church for the first time, I felt alone. I didn't know anyone here. I really didn't even know Lindy!

The bullying voice inside my head reappeared and grew louder the closer we got to the picnic area. "You don't belong here," it shouted. "These people aren't like you. They won't accept you!" I wanted to run back to the car and drive away, but I couldn't do that to Lindy. She was blissfully unaware of the battle going on inside my mind as we walked. And as much as I wanted to run, I could not justify abandoning this little girl who viewed me so differently than I viewed myself.

That day I discovered with certainty that Mormons are peculiar. Thinking back, I'd always known this. My dad had pounded this concept into my head since I was a little kid. He really did not like religion. But up until that day in the canyon, I didn't realize how odd they were! After a few minutes of everyone awkwardly mingling in an uncomfortable group, some- one suggested that we all play a game.

I'd played plenty of drinking games—one of which almost killed me-but I'd never played a game with a bunch of people that didn't end with me being plowed. Did normal people do this kind of thing? Were we really going to play a kid game in the middle of the mountains with a bunch of people we didn't know? The answer, it turned out, was yes.

And it got worse. This particular game involved asking and answering questions to establish who knew their daughter the best. I suspect Lindy felt as much dread as I did at the prospect of playing. After all, we were virtually strangers to each other, surrounded by dads and daughters who had lived and grown together for years. This was not going to end well.

Leaning over, I whispered to Lindy, "I'm sorry, this might be..." and then I shrugged my shoulders, sheepishly. Lindy didn't seem worried at all, though. Smiling up at me, she said, "Let's guess!" I was amazed at her enthusiasm and at the same time shocked that she didn't seem to care that we were about to be embarrassed in front of everyone in the group. I drew from her confidence. "Well, all right!" I said, and tried to relax as we awaited our turn.

There were around 10 questions, ranging from "what is your favorite color?" to "what is your least favorite subject in school?" We had to predict our partner's answers and write our predictions down on a piece of paper without consulting our partner. When the time came to reveal our predictions, the results were amazing. Lindy and I guessed nearly every question right! If I hadn't been there to witness it, I wouldn't have believed it myself.

Lindy guessed where I went to school. I guessed what her favorite food was. She nailed my favorite color (white). I got lucky predicting her least favorite class subject. After every correct guess, we gave each other a high five. The expression on her face as our luck held was a mixture of amazement and pure happiness. Lindy looked like she was on top of the world, and truthfully, I wasn't far behind.

This experience was quite different from my past party adventures. Not only was I not drunk or high, but I was not alone. I had a partner. At past gatherings, I might have been surrounded by other people, but I was there to fulfill my own cravings and needs.

The truth is that I was completely disconnected emotionally from anyone around me. At work, I traded my time for money and was surrounded by other people who were either doing the same or were only interacting with me so that they could get the substances they were craving. In general, people hadn't wanted to be around me unless there was something in it for them.

And why would they? Years of feeling angry and sorry for myself had made me a miserable person to be with. But today was different. I was with a group of people who, other than Lindy, didn't know my name. There was no alcohol, no drugs, and no pressure to be the craziest person in attendance.

Instead, we were a group of men playing a corny game with a bunch of little girls on a Wednesday night, and everyone seemed content to be there. It felt like an episode from The Twilight Zone-like I'd accidentally slipped into "Bizarro World" where things are the exact opposite of normal.

In fact, the scene was as far from my normal Wednesday evenings as I could imagine. Normally, Wednesday night found me either working at the bar or drinking alone at home. I'd usually get wasted, destroy something, feel sorry for myself, pass out, and wake up Thursday morning feeling like I'd been run over by a bus.

But this Wednesday there was none of that. This Wednesday I was at a picnic with an 11-year-old girl who thought I was someone special. Nobody was hunting for drugs or alcohol. No chairs were being tossed about in a frenzy of rage. No empty bottles of booze were being shattered over the fireplace mantel for no apparent reason. There wasn't even any urinating in the corner. Instead, on this particular Wednesday, we were all getting ready to have hot dogs and Kool-Aid.

Life is a series of pivotal moments. In basketball, I learned to change direction by pivoting my foot. Every moment of the game involves swiveling around searching for an open teammate or an open shot to the basket. I remember games where I actually pivoted around in a complete circle trying to find an open teammate.

Changing direction in life isn't so different, but rather than trying to find someone to pass the ball to, we're trying to find joy. Isn't that the meaning of life? To find happiness?

My behavioral changes began on a small scale with the four commitments I made to Bishop Taylor. They grew more and more significant with time. There is no blitzing the quarterback to achieve success in the game of life.

Research suggests that it takes 21 days to form a new good habit and 66 days to break a bad one. For years, I repeated a habit of being dishonest, manipulative, sneaky, devious and conniving. Along with that, I created a years-long habit of thinking negatively about myself. That way of thinking and behaving led to a miserable existence, and those habits definitely took longer than 66 days to change.

The first small positive pivot was actually telling Rich the truth about my life. It would have been easy to lie and say my life was dandy, but instead, I was honest with him. I swallowed a lot of pride in being honest with Rich. It wasn't easy. After that day, it took months of relapsing, over and over, and then practicing honesty with Bishop Taylor, over and over, before I began to see any changes in myself. Changing those bad habits was uncomfortable. And the discomfort, combined with the bully in my head, made drugs and alcohol that much more attractive to me—thus, my repeated relapses.

Relying on alcohol and drugs is a great way to "numb out," and that was how I had been handling stress and conflict for over a decade. The problem with "numbing out" is that the issues you want to avoid are still there when the high (or drunken stupor) wears off. But as the months wore on, I used substances less and less. As the months went on, I actually began dealing with my negative feelings instead of covering them up.

Every small daily decision to be sober and deal with the negative emotions was another small pivot. Telling Rich the truth—pivot. Meeting and being honest with the bishop for the first time—pivot. Praying and reading a verse of scriptures daily—pivot. Being honest with the bishop week after week—pivot, pivot, pivot. Eventually, those small changes of behavior landed me in front of that lemonade stand, where I chose to make an even larger turn in my life by practicing actual charity.

The Todd of 10 months ago would have scoffed at the idea of giving away money. But this was a new Todd. This Todd was a little girl's hero. In the past, I was the guy at the bar, getting wasted and waking up covered with puke, but today I was honest, good, caring, and about to enjoy some hot dogs and Kool-Aid with a bunch of dads with their daughters. On that Wednesday, at a picnic with a bunch of strangers, I began to feel something that had been absent from my life for longer than I could remember: I felt connected. I even felt joy. Turned out, Mormons weren't so bad after all.

Chapter Eleven
"Kairos Moment"

"In order to love who you are, you cannot hate the experiences that shaped you"

- Andrea Dykstra

Ever wonder why things happen in life? Many people take comfort in the phrase "everything happens for a reason." I'm not one of those people. Sometimes things that happen in life don't necessarily have a reason; they simply happen. And with those experiences, we grow and learn.

Did you hear that? Let me say it again: With every single experience in life—good and bad–we grow and learn. In fact, I believe we have no choice BUT to grow from what happens in our lives. Isn't that wonderful? With this belief in place, we are able to look back at every experience that caused us grief or pain and discover how we came out the other side stronger, wiser, and more resilient. With this understanding, life is happening for you instead of to you.

Of course, I didn't have this understanding in my youth, so I spent a lot of time and energy feeling sorry for myself. I was a victim of life. And if I wasn't feeling victimized by a particular situation, I would project victim status onto other people around me and feel sorry for them.

Victim thinking was such second nature to me that earlier during that pivotal picnic, I'd felt sorry for Lindy. Even before the matching game started, I apologized, thinking I was sure to cause embarrassment or that we'd fail somehow ... poor us. Lindy was the opposite. Instead of going into "poor us" mode, she stayed positive and focused on having fun. She viewed the game happening for us instead of to us.

I really worked up an appetite dominating the matching game with Lindy. Lucky for me, Mormons really know how to plan for a picnic. All around me were bags of chips, potato salads, bowls of green Jell-O, and, at the top of the food chain: hot dogs. The evening was well underway by then, and all the dads and daughters seemed to gravitate toward the food tables. Lindy and I were there too, but I wasn't going to be the one to dig in first. This wasn't my normal scene, so I hung back, waiting to follow someone more experienced into line. It's a good thing, too, because they asked for someone to pray before we started eating. Bizarre. I'd never said a prayer over food in my life. I didn't even know that was a thing. I remember thinking, "What, is there something wrong with the hot dogs?" It's funny to think about now, but the practice was completely foreign to me then.

I went along with the other dads. They folded their arms; I folded my arms. They closed their eyes and bowed their heads; I did the same. In time, everyone quieted, and from somewhere in the crowd, someone began to pray.

As prayers go, there wasn't anything special about this one. In fact, it was pretty simple. I mean, how eloquent can the prayer be when the whole reason for it is to bless hot dogs and Kool-Aid?

It began with "Dear Heavenly Father, thank you for this..."-and that's all I can remember. I've never had a vision or seen an angel, but I can say that I've heard the voice of God. As the words of the prayer faded away in my head, another, louder, voice took its place. With a clarity that I cannot express in writing, God simply said, "Todd, I am so proud of you. You made an impact on this girl's life that she'll never forget. You are in the right place. You are doing the right thing, and I love you."

Another Kairos moment. It felt like a wave of warm water slowly washing over me from head to toe, but instead of water, I felt enveloped in absolute love. Complete comfort. Perfect peace. It took less than 30 seconds to pray over the food, and at the end of that half-minute blessing, I was sobbing.

The spectacle did not go unnoticed, and I imagine the rest of the group was thinking, "It was only a blessing on the food, dude!"

Concerned, the group of men and daughters gathered around me with the question in their eyes, and one even voiced it: "Are you okay?" They all cared for me. No judgment, only concern.

Overwhelmed with everything going on and struggling to speak through my tears, I heard myself say, "I'm so sorry. These are happy tears." And then a fresh flood of those healing tears streamed down my face. In that moment, I made a choice: I was never going to use again. I was going to help kids like Lindy for the rest of my life. At that moment, I not only felt like I mattered, but I felt like I could actually make an impact on someone else's life.

And I realized, truly, that there was nothing wrong with me. Not only was I not broken or damaged, I never had been! I was always whole. Always complete. That realization would be the greatest treasure I took from that day. There was never anything wrong with me.

Along with that realization came the recognition that God had spoken to me! He actually existed and, however impossible, He knew me by name. I must have been in shock at this thought, because time didn't seem to flow like normal. Instead, it felt like a stone skipping over water with actual memory happening only when the rock came in contact with the water.

That's the best way to describe it.

I have no recollection of how long it took for the crowd of concerned people around us to disperse. They just eventually did. I don't recall Lindy's exact words to me as she stood by my side trying to console a blubbering twenty-something-year-old man. I only know she was there, and that alone was a comfort to me. I don't even remember when we all finally started to eat. In time, the moment passed and the group went on with the daddy-daughter picnic activities.

God had spoken to me! That realization kept coming back to me. He loved me. After everything I'd done, He still loved me. I had lived the life of an addict, I'd hurt my friends and family, I'd cheated, stolen and lied. But He still spoke to me. The more I thought about it, the more I realized that everything that had happened to that point in my life had happened for me. Every experience, both good and bad, had shaped the man I was at that moment. I wouldn't have even been at a picnic with a little 11-year-old girl had I not chosen my own, personal path of addiction.

Some could argue that it happened for a reason. I still don't believe that. I do believe, however, that it all happened for me, and that my past had prepared me for that moment. Your past is part of you—despising any part of it is like rejecting a part of yourself.

After the picnic, Lindy and I said our goodbyes to everyone and slowly walked to the car. I say "walked," but it was more like floating. I was higher than I'd ever been on drugs. Lindy seemed to sense that she'd been part of something special. I still remember that little girl's smile, her blue eyes beaming as I opened the door for her. Or maybe she was simply happy to have successfully attended her first daddy-daughter date. Who knows?

Chapter Twelve
"RecoverED"

" The words that follow '/ am' follow you"

There's always a decision to make after awareness occurs. The picnic with Lindy marked an experience that made me aware, without any doubt, that I was going in the right direction. Before the picnic, I believed I was broken and damaged. I believed I was a loser, an addict, a liar and a cheater.

The experience at the picnic provided me with an alternate belief system to pick up if I chose. According to this new belief system, I was a good person, someone who cared, someone who was honest, someone who was not broken-in fact, I was someone who wasn't even damaged. There was nothing wrong with me.

This new way of thinking told me that I had done bad things in the past, but today I was clean and sober. Today I was honest and kind. In this moment I was caring, intelligent, confident and likeable. Had I done some pretty ugly things for years and years? Yes. Did that make me a bad person? No.

As the days passed, the memory of hearing God's voice during that simple prayer was not as crystal clear as it had been the day it happened,

---

or the week after, but I still clung to my resolve never to do drugs again. I also knew that helping kids was important to me. Eventually, I found a way to combine my commitment to maintain sobriety and my desire to help children-but I'm jumping ahead. At this point in my story, I was white-knuckling it.

Not doing drugs and alcohol felt uncomfortable. I'd been in the dark for so long that being clean didn't feel normal; I wasn't used to it. I still had cravings-intense ones-for the substances that had gotten me through tough situations in the past. I realized that I needed to do something more than merely commit to myself in order to stay clean. I decided that maybe focusing my energy on something else besides thinking about not drinking would help. As I thought about it, I realized that thinking about not doing drugs seemed to bring on cravings almost as much as thinking about doing drugs.

I knew that I had to focus my energy somewhere else entirely because putting time and energy into thinking about drugs or alcohol in any way seemed only to fuel my desire to use. I needed help.

Thinking back, I remembered looking forward to my Saturday visits to Lindy's lemonade stand. When I was focused on the lemonade stand, I wasn't craving drugs or alcohol at all. Implementing this idea of redirecting thought and energy would be key in my recovery from addiction.

I tried to think of ways that I could help kids avoid the same mistakes I had made, but I couldn't come up with anything concrete. Ideas fluttered through my mind but never seemed to get a foothold-like a butterfly trying to land on a branch during a windy day; it comes close but then is blown off track and has to start over. This answer wasn't going to be gained easily. I would have to put in some effort. I decided to pray for guidance, ideas and direction. I still wasn't perfect at praying, and it still felt somewhat unnatural for me, but I kept at it.

By the time a month had passed since the picnic Kairos moment, prayer was becoming a powerful influence in my life. I felt more comfortable than ever not only praying for guidance, but also really believing that God was listening.

It's funny how life seems to fall into place when our behaviors are in line with who we are at our core. At my core, I had always been honest, genuine, caring and sensitive, but during the years I was using drugs, my behaviors didn't match my core. While using drugs, I was lying, stealing, manipulating, cheating and hurting those around me. Every person in addiction can attest that living a chaotic life results in a lot of negative consequences, which are a pretty handy excuse to continue using drugs. And the cycle goes on and on.

But my experiences with Lindy and the lemonade stand, as well as the insight that I had gained since my experience at the picnic, had made me realize that my behaviors didn't define who I was—the internal attributes at my core did. I wasn't a bad person. Rather, I was an honest, good person who had been behaving badly. See the difference?

Of course a person who believes they are bad or flawed will feel sad and hopeless. But I had learned the truth and had been able to realize that my behaviors, although bad, were separate from who I was at my core.

My life was changing for the better. Feelings of hope and contentment filled my days more and more-all because my thinking and behaviors were aligning more and more with my core self. It was around this time that the "butterfly" finally landed. My epiphany came during the era of Nancy Reagan's national "Just Say No" campaign. I was vaguely familiar with how it worked, mainly because it was right in the title. I loved that a leader of my country seemed to be on the same page I was and recognized the need to address children about the dangers of drugs and alcohol. The timing was perfect, and I wanted to get involved.

I needed more information about the program, but I also figured that knocking on the front door of the White House wasn't likely to produce the results I needed, so I opted to make a phone call. The "Just Say No" advertising campaign was championed by the First Lady, so it wasn't difficult to find the phone number.

My hope was that they might share with me some details of how the campaign functioned and, if I was lucky, I'd be able to figure out from there how to get involved. I started the call by requesting information on the "Just Say No" campaign at a local school. The representative on the other end of the line said that this was a grassroots effort for the First Lady, so they were accepting volunteers. If you could help spread the word, you had the job. I quickly expressed interest and was sent a packet of information about the program.

I looked up the closest elementary school to me and called the phone number. A polite woman listened patiently while I stammered through my pitch, explaining that I was part of Nancy Reagan's "Just Say No" campaign. Thankfully, she looked past my nervousness and gave permission for me to come present at a school assembly.

When I took a moment and thought about what I had signed up to do, I was amazed at myself. I-a former drug addict-was actually going to represent the United States' "War on Drugs" to a bunch of elementary school kids.

This would be the first of many speaking events for me. After the simple 30-minute presentation at the school assembly, I was bombarded by kids. They were so grateful and gracious that it immediately affirmed to me that this was what I needed to do. I was going in the right direction. The words I had heard during that prayer at the picnic echoed in my mind, "Todd, I am so proud of you. You made an impact on this girl's life that she'll never forget. You are in the right place. You are doing the right thing, and I love you."

I was going in the right direction, but I realized after that first presentation that I wanted to present the anti-drug information in my own way. The lights were on, the doors were opening, and I had clarity on the next step. To make this campaign truly mine, I would need to come up with my own slogan and a character who would connect with the kids and help me carry my message.

I sat down with a piece of paper and started doodling slogans and ideas for characters. Suddenly, the words "drug free, that's me" popped into my head. "Drug free, that's me." The phrase repeated over and over in my mind and settled there. At the same time, I realized that my doodle had begun to look like a dog-a stick-figure dog, but a dog nonetheless. On my third attempt at refining the figure, I knew for a certainty that I was looking at a dog, and by the fourth attempt, I could probably have convinced someone that they were looking at a dog. (I am not an artist, so this dog doodle may have been the biggest miracle of this story.) Feeling a surge of creativity, I gave the dog my nickname from high school, "Sly Dog."

Riding the high of inspiration and success after creating my character and my new slogan, I launched my plan to take my message to children. Within five short years, I had presented the message to over 100,000 elementary school students in the Salt Lake Valley.

Speaking events at the elementary schools led to speaking events at high schools. Speaking events at high schools led to requests from parents to talk with their teens who were struggling with addiction or self-esteem. Initially, I did this "life coaching" for free. A parent would ask me to talk to his or her child and I'd say, "Sure, I'll sit and talk to your kid." The more I served others, the more opportunities opened up. Long story short, I've been a motivational speaker for more than 20 years now and have addressed literally hundreds of thousands of kids.

It's incredible to me to think that all of this—my entire life-changing journey-began with seven words: "God, if you're there, I need help." From that one small pivot came more than 10,000 hours of individual counseling sessions with people of all ages and all walks of life. I have discovered that, in serving others, we help ourselves. Focusing on others helps me to remember who I am.

I've been clean now for 28 years, and I've never looked back. Well, that's not entirely true. I look back every time one of my childhood or adult friends dies by overdose or something related to alcohol. I look back and remember how close I was to having the same outcome and how grateful I am that, with God's help, I was able to turn my life around.

Everything starts with the power of thought. Ever heard the phrase "perception is reality"? Well, if that's true, we can change our reality by changing our perceptions. In other words, the way we perceive ourselves and the events in our lives can actually determine our reality. I choose to believe that the events of my life happened for me rather than to me. That is my perception of things.

When you look at the phrasing (life happening for me rather than to me) you'll see that only one word is different-but oh, what a difference that one word makes. Changing the word "to" to "for" switches the message from "you are a victim of life" to "you are empowered by life." I've learned and grown from every single experience in my life, exactly as you have from yours.

The wonderful little secret that very few people know is that we can't help but grow from the past. This is terrific news because we can't love who we are unless we learn to love where we came from. Our experiences, good and bad, have shaped us into the resilient, strong, willful, caring, understanding and wise humans we see in the mirror. Thank God for every little bit of our past.

"It's all in your head!" That's what my dad used to say when I voiced doubts or concerns about anything growing up. When I was a kid, this drove me nuts. Now, as a man who has learned the power of thoughts and perception, I teach this as a belief system to my own family. It is all in your head. The power to change your life is within you.

Ralph Waldo Emerson said, "You are what you think all day long." How different would life have been if that voice in my head had spent years telling me, "You are great, you are smart, you are confident, you are amazing," instead of the negative messages it actually gave me throughout my childhood and teenage years: "You're a loser, you're ugly, you're dumb, you're a nobody." That negative narration of thought led to low self-esteem, which then led to me trying to cover my self-doubt with mind-altering substances.

Because thinking is so powerful, it's imperative that we are aware of the words we tell ourselves. I read somewhere, "The words that follow 'I am,' follow you." Think about that. Whatever we tell ourselves we are, we are. Phrases like "I'm depressed" or "I'm anxious" or—my favorite—"I'm an addict" are self-fulfilling prophecies. We toss these phrases around in conversation with ourselves or with others without realizing the impact they are having.

By repeating such phrases over and over, we unconsciously pound out a narrative about ourselves and, in time, we begin to accept the identity that follows the words "I am." With every negative term that follows the words "I am" comes ownership. Are you really depressed, or is that simply how you're feeling right now? Are you really an anxious person at your very core, or is that something you've been labeled with because that's how you once felt temporarily? Am I really an addict—is that my identity? Or am I—at my core—a good person who is using drugs to cover up a lot of hurt? The underlying message of all this negative self-talk is really this: "I am damaged" or "I am broken" or "There's something wrong with me."

This message of being broken or damaged is rampant in our society in general, but the addiction community takes it to a whole different level with the phrase "I have a disease." I believe that this type of terminology hurts rather than helps people who are struggling. Repeated often enough, these words start attaching to your identity, and let me tell you from experience, it does not feel good.

Every part of life is good, even the bad. Why? Because our struggles give us strength. Life has taught me many things. The most important truth, though, is that there's nothing wrong with me. There never was. I was always OK. I was never broken or damaged. Even at the height of my addictive behaviors, I was always me: honest, kind, caring, and compassionate.

My actions were simply so out of alignment with who I was that it resulted in a ton of negative emotion. Isn't it wild to think that my thoughts created my perceptions, which created my reality? I was always in control of my own reality—I simply didn't know it. Thinking creates feeling, not the other way around. We think and then we feel and then we behave according to that feeling.

What tripped me up and created the depression that almost caused me to stick a shotgun in my mouth was what I believed about myself. I had spent so long repeating the narrative "I am worthless, a loser, a liar, a cheater, a thief" that I came to believe that I was all those things. But I wasn't. And neither are you. You have your own false stories that you tell yourself, but I'm here to challenge those narratives. There's nothing wrong with you, exactly like there was nothing wrong with me. At our core, we are good.

Every bit of my life has happened for me. After the experience at the picnic with Lindy, it didn't take long to become an active member of The Church of Jesus Christ of Latter-day Saints-aka the LDS, or Mormon, church. A few years after turning my life around, I married a beautiful woman, and together we've raised a family. Now it's my kids' turn to hear their dad say, "It's all in your head!"

If there's anything I would want them to know, it's that they are more special than they realize. We all are. The late Neal A. Maxwell, a member of the Quorum of the Twelve Apostles of my church, said it best: "Think of it, brothers and sisters, even with their extensive longevity, stars are not immortal, but you are." The message is this: We are priceless, and nothing we do or say can change our value. Ever.

Epilogue
"When Life Gives You Lemons"

It's not every day that you meet someone who will change your life forever. Only every so often do we get a glimpse at how God works with his mysterious ways. Rarely are his methods very straightforward. Rather, they are more often presented the way a parable would be, giving me the opportunity to understand him at the pace I'm prepared for …

A father is more of a biological term than a role or relationship. A dad is someone who is present.

This is a letter I received from Lindy, a young friend who turned out to be key in my recovery.

I am an only child raised by my mother – it has just been me and her for most of my life. She is the greatest mother a child could ever ask for, who has dedicated her life to my happiness; she is my best friend. Despite the fact that I have the best mom in the world, even as a young child I always wished and hoped for a dad. Each night I would pray to God to send us a dad to take care of us and make our family complete. It wasn't until quite recently – now an adult – I was able to recognize my prayers were answered all those years ago.

When I was around 8 years old, I asked my mom for a trampoline. It was the only thing in the world that I wanted almost as much as I wanted a daddy. She told me that we could not afford one, so I told her that I would earn the money and pay for it myself. Then she told me that if we got a trampoline, we would need to put a fence around it that we also could not afford, so I told her that I would earn the money and pay for that too.

With the help of my mom, I set up a lemonade stand on the street next to our house. I was determined to get that trampoline. It wasn't long before an extremely handsome guy pulled up to my stand and asked me how much for a lemonade. After I said a cup of lemonade would be 25 cents, he reached down and grabbed the biggest handful of quarters, nickels and dimes I had ever seen and dumped them in my hands! I had struck it rich and was grinning from ear to ear as I ran right into my house to tell my mom what had just happened. Not only was this guy very generous, he was also very good-looking and became an instant crush. This same guy came back several times and each time gave me all the coins he could find in his car for a cup of my lemonade. This meant so much to me as a little girl.

A short while later, I was at church with my mother when I recognized this same guy from my lemonade stand. I could not believe my eyes. I grabbed a mirror from my mother's purse so that I could secretly look back at him the entire meeting.

Later we had a church-organized daddy-daughter date for all of the youth to go up in the mountains to play games and roast hot dogs around a fire. Feeling devastated, I did not know what to do since I did not have a dad to bring. Todd came to my mind, and at that moment I knew I wanted to take him as my daddy-daughter date. My mom tracked down and asked him if he would come and be my daddy for the night. To our surprise, he said yes! I could not have been more excited.

This much-anticipated night finally arrived, and he picked me up and we drove up to the mountains together. Just like any first date, I remember him opening my door for me and on the drive up the canyon he was so kind and charming, asking lots of questions, wanting to get to know me better.

One of the planned activities was a newlywed-style game to find out which daddy-daughter pairs knew each other best. Despite our unconventional situation, we actually won! It turned out we hit all the right questions on our short drive up the canyon. I felt like the luckiest girl in the world, and the night turned out perfect.

Time passed, and a couple years later I was still attending Quail Hollow Elementary School in Sandy, Utah. They announced that we had a special weeklong anti-drug presentation coming called Sly Dog.

It turns out I couldn't shake him – this same wonderful man had resurfaced in my life and was the presenter of this fun, memorable and influential program. He played basketball with us and even had a mascot – however, my favorite part was probably the pizza party we had at the end. He spent an entire week with us, teaching us the importance of saying no to drugs. In my eyes he was famous, and I was so proud to know him.

Around this same time a school-sponsored daddy-daughter date was approaching. It was a roller-skating party at Classic Fun Center, and everyone was going. Once again, I asked my mom if Todd could please be my dad. She reached out to him, and he agreed to come and take me. I was so excited I could hardly wait for the night to come. When he picked me up, I couldn't help but feel so lucky to have him as my date. He was an excellent skater and I got to skate with him the whole night. I even got to hold his hand! Not everyone was as elated as I was. While visiting the ladies' room, I overheard some girls ask, "Why does that girl get to keep skating with Sly Dog?" not realizing that he was my date. I was on cloud nine the entire night spending time with the best dad a girl could ever hope for! He was my hero. I even wrote about him in my fifth grade autobiography as the person that I admired the most.

More time passed, and my sophomore year of high school my mother decided to write him a letter thanking him for his kindness to let him know what he did for our small family. He was our angel. He gave me a gift that I had always desired and was able to fill the role of the father I never had! Some time later Todd sent a letter mentioning that the first daddy-daughter date he went on with me had a huge impact on his life and that it was a turning point in his decision to turn his life around. We'd had no idea that he was impacted by our meeting each other.

While studying at the University of Utah, Todd requested an interview from me to help him make a movie for his program, Sly Dog - Drug Free That's Me, that he was taking nationwide. We met at the same elementary school (also located on the same street that we met) and I got to share how the Sly Dog program helped me make good choices. I remember how impressed I was by his dedication to helping others make wise decisions.

About a year ago Todd resurfaced yet again in my life - over 10 years since I had last seen him, and over 25 years since we had first met that day at the lemonade stand. A man we knew had heard him speak, and he told my mom that we were a huge part of his story, saying, "Your daughter is the lemonade stand girl." This same man called to inform us that Todd would be speaking the following Saturday at a conference in a building on the same street where we had met - just a few blocks from where I used to set up my lemonade stand. He insisted that we be there to hear his story.

Todd did not know that we would be there, and when he saw us all three of us he could not fight back the tears at this incredible reunion. This was the first time I had ever heard his full side of the story. Tears filled my eyes the entire time he was speaking; who knew that the guy who had changed the course of my life forever felt the exact same way about me? My entire life I always thought that Todd was my angel, but it turns out we were each other's. That one moment in time changed everything!

Todd may not have realized the impact he had on me that day at the lemonade stand. He may have given me a few bucks toward my trampoline. But what he really gave me was the greatest gift of all - an answer to countless prayers and the dad I never had! I now have a deepened under-standing of this phrase: "When life gives you lemons, make lemonade."

- Lindy Davis

About the Author

Todd currently serves as a Mentor & Personal-Development Coach for those looking to get more out of life, and he also works at, what he calls the best University on the Planet, Wasatch Recovery Treatment Center as a Belief System Counselor.

In 1989 he founded the non-profit, anti-drug entity Sly Dog "Drug Free That's Me, which features a sought-after education program for ele- mentary schools. This program has encouraged over 100 thousand school-age students, emphasizing principles of positive self- talk, personal commitment, goal setting, and character building.

Todd spent his youth addicted to drugs and alcohol. Through his own recovery and newfound awareness, Todd learned that more powerful than any addiction was the power of the human soul. Over the past 25 years Todd has discovered and taught universal principles that have empowered thousands to conquer addiction, crush compulsive behaviors and change their limiting belief systems.

Todd's story was recently told through a popular YouTube clip that received over 1 million views and has been translated into 3 languages. Todd has conducted over 1,000 speaking engagements and close to 10,000 individual coaching sessions.

Todd is an author of the popular eBook "It's Time to Start Living" available on Amazon. He also produces a popular Podcast on iTunes that he actually calls a Beliefcast that is geared toward high school and middle school aged kids.

Todd's Story was also featured in Best Selling Author Simon Sinek's new book, "Find Your Why".

Today, Todd uses his firsthand fight against addiction to give hope to thousands of teenagers, young adults, parents and connects with them on an authentic level.

Todd has been married to his sweetheart for 27 years. They have four children and live a happy, busy life together.

Here are some links for more information about Todd...
Website: http://www.toddsylvesterinspires.com/
iTunes: https://itunes.apple.com/us/podcast/todd-sylvester-in-spires-beliefcast/id1333144561?mt=2
YouTube Channel: http://www.youtube.com/c/ToddSylvester
Facebook: https://www.facebook.com/TSinspires

CPSIA information can be obtained
at www.ICGtesting.com
Printed in the USA
FSHW020238160421

9 781513 655765